BRITAIN'S
CANALS

In memory of Peter White,
canal architect and good friend

BRITAIN'S CANALS

EXPLORING THEIR ARCHITECTURAL AND ENGINEERING WONDERS

Text by Anthony Burton

Photography by Derek Pratt

ADLARD COLES

LONDON · OXFORD · NEW YORK · NEW DELHI · SYDNEY

ADLARD COLES
Bloomsbury Publishing Plc
50 Bedford Square, London, WC1B 3DP, UK

BLOOMSBURY, ADLARD COLES and the Adlard Coles logo
are trademarks of Bloomsbury Publishing Plc

First published in Great Britain 2020

A catalogue record for this book is available from the
British Library

Library of Congress Cataloguing-in-Publication data has
been applied for

ISBN: PB: 978-1-4729-7195-1; ePDF: 978-1-4729-7194-4;
eBook: 978-1-4729-7192-0

10 9 8 7 6 5 4 3 2 1

Designed and typeset in Franklin Gothic by
Louise Turpin

Printed and bound in India by
Replika Press Pvt. Ltd.

To find out more about our authors and
books visit www.bloomsbury.com and sign
up for our newsletters

PAGE 1: The old glass works cone looms over the
Stourbridge Canal.
PAGE 2/3: The canal basin at Stourport.
ABOVE: Maintenance workers on the drained locks
at Bingley on the Leeds & Liverpool Canal.
BELOW: The Rochdale Canal at Hebden Bridge.

CONTENTS

INTRODUCTION

The canals of Great Britain are probably busier today than they have been at any time in the last 100 years. Where once it was the bustling traffic of working barges and narrow boats, today it is holidaymakers who fill our waterways. But it is the working days that give the canals their unique character and appeal. We are fortunate that the great age of canal construction, from 1760 to the early years of the 19th century, coincided with one of the greatest periods of British architecture – the Georgian age. Many of the buildings that were erected for strictly commercial purposes have the same air of quiet dignity and good proportion that characterised that time. There is, however, more to it than that. Because different companies built the individual canals and hired different architects and engineers, each canal has its own distinctive features. For example, leaving the gentle meanderings of James Brindley's Staffs and Worcester Canal for the ruthlessly direct line of Thomas Telford's Shropshire Union Canal is to enter a wholly different world.

In this book, we have tried to show in words and pictures all the different elements that combine to give the canals their special appeal to so many of us. Often it seems it is the very simplest structures that carry the strongest message. Such as it is impossible to imagine our canals without the gentle curves of a stone or brick bridge, or structures that have only mellowed with age. We tend to think of our canals as being part of a bygone age, which indeed they are and that is part of their charm. But in their day, they were at the very forefront of technological change and at the heart of the Industrial Revolution. Before the canal age, it would have been impossible to even imagine mass-producing bridges, for example. Yet that is exactly what the Horseley Iron Company did when they created the iron bridges that can be seen throughout the Birmingham canal system, masterpieces of innovation and elegance. Our hope is that readers will come away with a new appreciation of the historic structures that give our canals their unique character.

OPPOSITE: The spectacular locks at Foxron on the Leicester line of the Grand Union Canal. There are two five-lock staircases, in which one lock is joined directly to the next: this view is looking up to the second staircase, with its neat, vernacular lock cottage at the top.

CHAPTER 1

SETTING THE LINE

Before work could begin on constructing a canal, there were essential decisions to be taken. The chief engineer had to work out exactly where it was to be built – lay down the precise line it would have to follow. In a totally flat landscape, there would be no problem. All the engineer would need to do would be to draw a straight line between the two ends, dig a ditch along that line and make it watertight. But the British landscape is rarely flat, and this is particularly true of the areas where new industries were being developed – areas most in need of improved transport. They were marked by hills and valleys, humps and hollows. There were two basic approaches to tackling the problem. The engineer could avoid it altogether by trying to remain on the flat, following the natural contours of the land – contour cutting. Or alternatively he could tackle the issue head on, charging through hills in cuttings and tunnels and crossing valleys on high banks and aqueducts.

Contour cutting

In the early years of canal construction, a network was developed in the Midlands, known as 'The Grand Cross', that was to unite four great rivers – the Trent, the Mersey, the Severn and the Thames. All these canals made extensive use of contour cutting and the chief engineer responsible for each of them was James Brindley. He had made his reputation when he was invited by the Duke of Bridgewater to work on his canal, the first in Britain to be built that was independent of any natural waterway. When it opened in 1761, it attracted a great deal of interest, not just from the merely curious but from industrialists eager to improve transport for their own concerns. Brindley had shared the work on the Bridgewater Canal with the duke and, one of his agents, John Gilbert, and they remained working for the duke. It made Brindley man of the moment – everyone wanted him as their engineer. His dictum was that he could conquer water by 'laying it on its back' – in other words, keeping the canal on the same level for as long as possible, even if that involved indulging in extravagant loops and curves.

Today we can get a good idea of the nature of any landscape simply by looking at an Ordnance Survey map, where the contour lines clearly define the rise and fall of the land. But that great project for mapping the whole of Britain only began in the 1780s, by which time Brindley was dead – so when that engineer began planning his routes, he had no maps to guide him. Instead, he set off on his horse on what he called an 'ochilor survey' or a 'ricconitring' (ocular survey). In other words, he trotted over the route on horseback to get a general idea of the lie of the land so that plans could be drawn up. One of the most extravagantly convoluted sections of canal can be found on the southern part of the Oxford Canal at Wormleighton – anyone travelling by boat might look across and see another that appears to be travelling towards them, but in fact is heading the same way. It just happens to be on the opposite side of a great curve, which almost turns the house on top of the low hill into a moated manor.

The northern section of this canal is quite different, following a very direct line, but it was not always like that. It was, like the southern section, a meandering waterway, and boatmen would complain that they could travel all day and still hear Brinklow clock strike the hours. But later on, following the construction of the Grand Junction Canal, this part became a vital link in the route between London and Birmingham. As a result, a major improvement programme was set under way. At Newbold, anyone going for a walk in the fields near the present canal can find the curious sight of canal bridges standing forlornly, crossing nothing more significant than an indentation in the ground (all that remains of Brindley's original), while beside the church there is still the entrance to the first tunnel, on a totally different line from the one in use today. It is a dramatic indication of just how wayward the old line was.

A similar story can be told about the Birmingham Canal, linking the city to Wolverhampton. Once again, a new straight main line was constructed, but this

PREVIOUS PAGE: Contour cutting on the Leeds and Liverpool – the canal swings in an extravagant curve round the hillock.

time the old was not abandoned, simply because important industries had grown up alongside it. For example, the famous builders of steam engines, Boulton and Watt, had established their factory, the Soho works, by the canal and relied on it for transport, so the old line remained in use, now becoming the Soho Loop.

It was not only on the Brindley canals that contour cutting was used. The central Pennine section of the Leeds and Liverpool Canal has bends that are every bit as extravagant as any in the Midlands. And there are canals where following the contours is the only viable option. The Brecon and Abergavenny Canal runs through the Brecon Beacons National Park and at its eastern end starts on the hillside, high above the Usk Valley. As it winds its way round the Blorenge hill, it necessarily follows every fold in the land, and at one point has to turn through a complete horseshoe bend. And even on canals that in general take a more direct approach, there may still be sections where staying on the level through twists and turns has been considered the best option.

Cut and fill

Contour cutting dominated the early years, but as engineers became more confident they began to use extensive earthworks to tackle obstacles. A new technique was developed, known as 'cut and fill'. Deep cuttings were carved through hills and the spoil used to build up embankments across the next valley. There are many places where this can be seen, but none shows the technique more dramatically than the Birmingham and Liverpool Junction Canal, on which construction began in 1825, right at the end of the canal construction age. Here, cuttings such as Woodseaves and Grub Street are deep gashes in the land, while banks such as Sheldon ride high above the surrounding countryside.

A typical straight, deep cutting on the Shropshire Union Canal at Woodseaves.

Cut and fill was not the only possible response to hilly country. The first trans-Pennine canal, the Leeds and Liverpool, took a huge sweep to the north to avoid the problem. The two canals that followed took the direct approach, charging up one side of the Pennine hills in a steady procession of locks and dropping down the other with still more. The Rochdale actually originally had 92 locks in just 32 miles (51km) of canal. The Huddersfield not only has 74 locks, but in the centre of the hills there is Britain's longest canal tunnel, the Standedge.

These different approaches to construction give the modern canal traveller, boating for pleasure, quite different experiences. The contour canals can seem almost like natural waterways as they meander gracefully through the countryside. With cut and fill there is no escaping that this is an artificial waterway, but it can also be very dramatic. Deep in the cutting, one can seem to be in a secret world of one's own, while the banks provide panoramic views. The heavily locked canals can take the holidaymaker to some magnificent scenery, but at the cost of a lot of hard work. Each type of canal has its own appeal, setting the overall pattern of travel. But that is just the broad picture. Much of the pleasure of canal travel comes from the fact that each canal has its own unique character. This largely comes from the way in which all the different features are handled – and it is these features we shall be looking at in detail in the following chapters.

LEFT: A lock on the Caldon Canal, a short but very attractive waterway.

BELOW: This old map shows part of the original main line of the Bridgewater Canal, wriggling its way across the landscape.

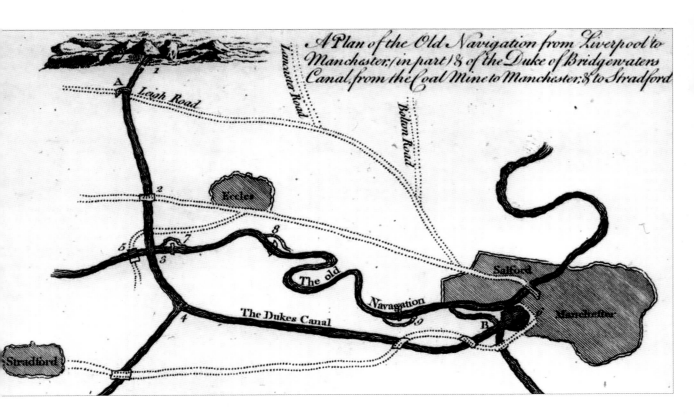

The engineers

The work of two engineers typifies the two main approaches: James Brindley was the main protagonist for contour cutting, Thomas Telford for cut and fill.

Brindley was born in Derbyshire in 1716, received virtually no formal education and as soon as he

ABOVE: The summit lock on the Rochdale Canal – the waterway has climbed to the top of the Pennines.

was old enough was apprenticed to a millwright. Just 20 years later he had set up in business for himself at Leek in Staffordshire. He built a mill there, which now houses the Brindley Museum.

His reputation grew over the years, and he was involved in projects for draining collieries, which included the aptly named Wet Earth mine. This involved providing a long underground channel, in effect a small canal. It was this success that brought him to the attention of the Duke of Bridgewater. From then on canals would occupy all his time, endlessly travelling from one proposed canal site to another, working out the best route that would involve the least earthworks. His greatest achievement was the creation of The Grand Cross, linking four great rivers of England, via the Trent and Mersey, the Staffordshire and Worcestershire, the Coventry and the Oxford canals. Exhausted by his work, and suffering from diabetes, he died in 1772.

Thomas Telford was born in Eskdale in the Scottish Lowlands in 1757, the son of a shepherd. Like Brindley, he was apprenticed at an early age to a stonemason, but managed to acquire an education in his spare time – he was an enthusiastic amateur poet. To gain further experience, he travelled first to Edinburgh to work on the New Town, then to London where he was employed in the construction of Somerset House. He was gifted and ambitious. He attracted the attention of Sir William Pulteney, allegedly the richest man in Britain, who gave him the task of renovating Shrewsbury Castle, and then used his influence to have Telford appointed County Surveyor for Shropshire, during which time he designed two churches, at Bridgnorth and Madeley. He might well have had a career as a competent but uninspiring architect had he not been appointed to the Ellesmere Canal. He was fortunate to have a mentor in the very competent William Jessop, and to have arrived on the scene when new technologies made earthworks on a massive scale feasible. Without the use of steam power, the great project of the Caledonian Canal would have been impossible. His work on the new line of the Birmingham Canal and the Shropshire Union represents the embodiment of cut and fill. He was not limited to canal work, having also been involved in dock and harbour construction, including St Katharine Docks in London. He served as the first president of the Institution of Civil Engineers from 1820 until his death in 1834.

PLACES TO VISIT

WORSLEY DELPH: Worsley, Manchester M28 2GD: The start of the Bridgewater Canal, where the story begins!

BRINDLEY'S MILL AND THE JAMES BRINDLEY MUSEUM: A523 between Leek and Macclesfield ST13 8FA.

OXFORD CANAL WINDING ROUND WORMLEIGHTON HILL: Footpath from the church, Wormleighton CV47 2XH.

LEEDS AND LIVERPOOL CANAL CONTOUR CUTTING: Greenberfield Locks, Greenberfield Lane, Barnoldswick BB18 5SU.

SOHO LOOP: The original line of the Birmingham Canal, Foundry Lane, Smethwick B66 2LL.

CHAPTER 2

LOCKS AND LOCK COTTAGES

The story of the canal lock goes back much further than the start of the canal age. Rivers had been important trade routes for centuries. In medieval times, the Severn was known as the King's Highway of Severn. Rivers, however, had always presented problems by not always flowing in a steady, convenient manner to suit boatmen. Sometimes they dashed along through rapids, while elsewhere they might spread out in languid shallows.

Even greater problems were caused by other river users. Millers needed river water to turn their waterwheels, and to ensure a steady supply they built weirs across the whole width of the waterway. These ensured a good head of water that could then be diverted through a leat to work their machinery, but cargo and passenger boats found their way blocked. The 'Water-Poet', John Taylor, wrote a verse account of a journey he made in the 17th century down the Thames from Oxford, and complained bitterly about the millers:

> *How can that man be called a good liver*
> *Who for his private use will stop a river?*

Flash locks

There was, however, a solution, the flash lock. Essentially, this was a gate let into the weir, which contained removable vertical planks. When these were lifted, the water would begin to flow through and the whole gate could be opened, allowing a rush of water to escape – the flash. Boats travelling downstream could ride the flash, while those travelling in the opposite direction would be winched up against the current. It was far from an ideal system, as was tragically demonstrated at Goring on the Thames when a passenger boat was overturned in the flash with loss of life.

LEFT: The first pound locks were closed by gates that were lifted vertically, as at this so-called guillotine lock at King's Norton junction.

ABOVE: The last surviving flash lock on the Thames at Eynsham survived long enough to be photographed.

Pound locks

The progression was the pound lock, so called because it impounded the water, but over the years the device has simply become the lock.

In its essentials, the lock consists of a waterproof chamber, closed by movable gates at either end fiitted with a system for letting water in and out. In the earliest versions, the lock gates that closed off both ends were raised and lowered vertically. This was a cumbersome system that involved the construction of a framework to keep the gates moving in a straight line and a complex system of wheels and pulleys to ease the work of lifting. Known originally as portcullis locks and later, for obvious if macabre reasons, as guillotine locks, they were rarely used on British canals. One surviving example is the stop lock that separates the Stratford Canal from the Worcester and Birmingham at King's Norton. It seems obvious to us today that this is very clumsy compared with the swinging lock gates with which we are

all familiar, but there was a problem that had to be overcome before the present system could come into use.

If one thinks of a boat approaching a lock that will take it down to a lower level, then it does not require the gate to reach to the bottom of the lock. All it needs is sufficient depth of water to float in, so the top lock gate can be shortened by resting it on a sill. This means it can easily be moved by using the balance beam. But if the bottom end is closed by a single gate, it will require a major effort to shift it. The obvious answer is to use double gates, but that is where the fresh difficulty appears. If they simply meet in a straight line, the water pressure will tend to force them apart. The solution was found by the artistic and engineering genius Leonardo da Vinci, who was appointed to plan the construction of Italy's Naviglio Interno. He set the gates to meet at an angle, like a mitre joint – hence the usual name of mitre gates. The V-shape pointed into the lock, so that water pressure tended to force them together instead of pushing them apart.

Gate paddles

Now that gates could be opened and closed with comparative ease, the next item to be considered was how to let water into and out of the lock. This could be done by having openings in the gates with movable covers – gate paddles – or by constructing culverts between the lock and the canal itself, covered by ground paddles inside the lock. The mechanism for moving the paddles varies enormously, with different engineers having their own ideas on the best design – this variation is just one of the factors that gives each canal its own unique character.

One of the simplest systems can be found on some of the locks on the Leeds and Liverpool Canal. Known as 'Jack Cloughs', the openings are covered by paddles attached to long handles, which are pulled down to act as levers to move the paddles. By far the most common system is the simple ratchet worked by a key – a portable handle – that fits on to the spindle to raise and lower the paddle.

There is something very satisfactory about this system when it works well and smoothly, with a comforting rattle. It is simple but practical and, apart from anything else, gives an instant visual indication of whether the paddle is raised or lowered (although the basics retain the same design, details vary). It all adds to the richness of the canal scene.

In recent years, many of the old gears have been replaced by hydraulic gears, which sit as rather bulbous excrescences on the beams. They are said to be easier to use but that is only because the old gears were not always regularly serviced. To my mind, the loss of the old gears has removed some of the attractive variety of the scene.

BOTTOM LEFT: The typical paddle gear used for winding the paddles up and down, to let water into and out of the lock chamber.

BELOW TOP: Unusual paddle gear on the Montgomery Canal.

BELOW BOTTOM: The gate paddle gear on a lock on the Worcester and Birmingham Canal silhouetted against the evening sky.

Weirs

The majority of locks also have some means of allowing excess water to bypass them. If the area above the lock fills up, perhaps after heavy rain, it can escape down the side via an overspill weir. These can be quite elaborate affairs. Those on the Macclesfield Canal are beautifully constructed of stone setts, while on other waterways, including the Staffs and Worcester, there are circular weirs through which the water disappears as through a bath plughole.

In fact, the more you look at locks, the more you come to appreciate their rich diversity. Though everything is done for strictly practical reasons, the effect can be almost sculptural. At many locks, the paving at the side has quarter circles of raised stone or brick beneath the balance beams, which give extra purchase for the feet as the boatman leans his weight against the beam.

Locks punctuate a voyage, with their wooden beams in crisp black and white contrasting with the spiky iron of paddle gear, all set off by mature stone and brickwork – a study in contrasting shapes and textures.

BELOW: A necessary addition to canal locks was a weir to take excess water round the lock instead of flooding over it. This unusual round weir is on the Staffs and Worcester Canal.

ABOVE: This lock on the Chesterfield Canal shows the brick quadrant, with raised brick ridges that help anyone opening and closing the gate to get a good grip for their feet.

LEFT: The stone steps have been worn down by countless feet. The simple footbridge at the tail of the lock is held on iron brackets.

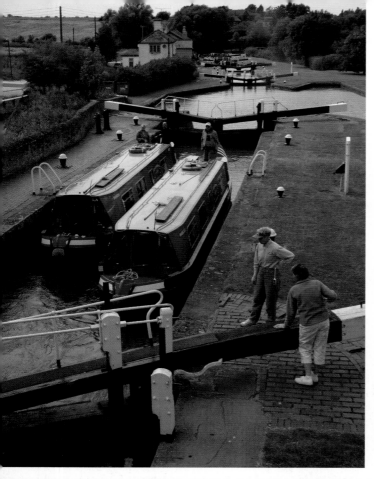

Different types of lock

Locks do more than simply allow boats to move up and down. They also determine the maximum size of craft that can use the waterway. We tend to think of Britain's canals in terms of the familiar narrow boat – the working boats on which most modern pleasure boats are based – but the earliest canal locks were based on existing vessels already in use on the local river, and they were generally broad-beamed barges.

The first lock in Britain to make use of mitre gates was ambitious – the Exeter Ship Canal.

TOP: The locks on the Grand Union Canal are able to take either a broad-beam barge or two narrow boats side by side. This was particularly useful in the 20th century, when boats worked as a pair with a motor boat towing an unpowered 'butty'. This lock is at Soulbury.

BOTTOM: A broad lock on the Leeds and Liverpool Canal at Johnson's Hillocks.

The route from the sea up the River Exe was blocked by a massive weir, the Countess Weir. In 1563, the citizens of Exeter obtained an Act of Parliament authorising a canal to bypass the weir that would allow seagoing vessels to reach the heart of the city. The engineer on the project was John Trew. All we know of him is that he came from Glamorgan, and that he constructed a massive lock joining the canal to the estuary – 189 feet (58m) long and 23 feet (7m) wide – and that the double mitre gate contained six sluices. There was always a problem constructing large lock chambers that could withstand the pressure of water on the inside and the earth outside. Trew's lock was turf-sided, but has long since been replaced (though the name 'Turf' lives on in the lock-side pub). Other turf locks have, however, survived.

TOP: The turf-sided lock at Garston on the Kennet Navigation; the iron rails prevent boats drifting on to the sloping sides.

BOTTOM: The top of the Tyrley flight on the Shropshire Union Canal. Like most narrow locks this one has double gates at the lower level and a singe gate at the top.

'The Kennet Navigation' was authorised in 1715. The Kennet falls so steeply that 18 locks were needed to overcome the change in level and were set in over 11 miles (18km) of artificial cutting. Two turf-sided locks remain in use. The upper sides of the lock slope outwards and are covered with turf. As the water rises it spreads gently outwards, while guide rails keep boats centred rather than drifting away to the side. An alternative way to resist pressure is by using an arch instead of a straight wall. Pierre-Paul Riquet, the pioneering engineer of the Canal du Midi in France, found difficulty in preventing lock walls from collapsing so he rebuilt them with curved sides, so that the locks are more or less elliptical in plan. One Kennet lock has adopted the idea, but instead of curved walls it has ones made of a series of arches, so that it appears to have a scalloped edge. By the 1760s, however, engineers were confidently building with straight walls of stone or brick. This was an advance, but in the Midlands there was a retrograde step: instead of the broad locks of the river navigations, there was a system based on narrow locks, which limited cargo-carrying capacity.

When the Bridgewater Canal was extended to the Mersey at Runcorn, locks were built to take the barges then in use on the river, the Mersey flats, roughly 70 feet (21m) long and 14 feet (4m) beam. As the Bridgewater was to be part of a greater network, it would have been sensible to keep these dimensions for the other linking canals, but when it came to the Trent and Mersey, the engineer, James Brindley, found an obstacle he simply could not go round – Harecastle Hill. His only option was to pierce it with a tunnel; however, he found the prospect of digging a tunnel that would be over a mile long (1.6km) and able to take 14-foot beam vessels simply too daunting, so he designed it for a 7-foot (2m) beam instead. In effect, that meant that 14-foot barges would not be able to use the canal, so there was no point in building wide locks.

BELOW: Somerton deep lock on the Oxford Canal is typical of the Midland canal system developed by Brindley, designed to take a 70-foot (21m) narrow boat.

From this one decision, the narrow lock and the narrow boat came to dominate the Midland system.

In other parts of Britain, canals were being built that, at the time, were never intended to link in with the Brindley network so the same restrictions didn't apply.

The Leeds and Liverpool Canal, for example, was built for wide barges, but the locks were only able to take vessels 60 foot (18m) long, which proved inconvenient later when links were made to canals to the south. In Scotland, however, there were no restrictions and the engineer John Smeaton could build the Forth and Clyde with generously sized locks. Although these canals were designed to take quite large vessels, lock design was not fundamentally different from that of the narrow canal. Towards the end of the canal age, more ambitious canals were built to take seagoing ships. The Caledonian ran right across Scotland and was originally designed to take vessels that included naval warships up to 160 feet (49m) long and 36 feet (11m) beam. The locks needed massive gates,

ABOVE: The sea lock at Ardrishaig. The vessel is leaving the Crinan Canal and entering Loch Fyne.

too heavy to be moved by conventional means. Today the system has been electrified, but one can still see the capstans that were used originally. They have sockets to allow long poles to turn them and they wound or unwound cables attached to the gates. The Caledonian is also one of a number of canals that have locks providing access to the sea.

An interesting feature is the sea lock at the Inverness end of the Caledonian Canal. The bay here has a very gently sloping shoreline, which means that ships cannot approach close to the land. So, as the ships could not reach the canal, the canal had to be thrust out to meet the ships. An embankment was built out into the sea and the channel and lock chamber then cut into it. It may not be the most spectacular feature of this canal, but it was a major work of engineering.

The 29-lock flight at Caen Hill near Devizes on the Kennet and Avon Canal had been derelict for years but has now been restored to its former glory.

Another intriguing sea lock can be seen on the Bude Canal in Cornwall. It juts out on to the sandy beach and is only usable at high tide.

Most locks are designed to overcome changes in level but there are exceptions. Canal companies often had to go to considerable expense to secure water supplies to feed the locks. The last thing they wanted was that same water being used for other canals, especially if no fees were involved. The answer was the stop lock – a shallow lock at a junction. It ensured that only a small quantity of water was passed on. The stop lock on the Worcester and Birmingham was so successful at keeping supplies from reaching the Birmingham Canal that it was known as the Worcester Bar.

Travellers coming north on the Oxford Canal from the city will come across a very strange-looking lock. Instead of the normal rectangular chamber, this one is hexagonal with only a slight rise and fall. In fact, when leaving the lock, boats will be temporarily changing from the canal and moving out on to the waters of the River Cherwell. At this point, river and canal are at almost the same level.

If a conventional lock had been built, not enough water would be passed through to feed the rest of the canal, hence the odd shape. The lock makes up in width what it lacks in depth. After this brief excursion on to the river, the canal is rejoined.

By now it should be obvious that locks come in a fascinating mixture of size and design, with different canals having their own distinct quirks and features. However, the character of a canal is not just distinguished by its individual designs, but to an even greater extent by the way in which they are organised.

On most of the early canals, locks tended to be spread out evenly along the whole length of the waterway, but as engineers got bolder and were prepared to tackle more formidable obstacles, it became necessary to group them together in long flights. These can be very impressive – and for anyone arriving by boat, quite daunting. For many years, the most imposing flight was at Hatton on the Grand Union.

The locks are very different from the originals constructed in the 1790s. In 1929, the old Grand

BELOW: The Hatton flight of 21 locks is a daunting sight. The covered paddle gear was installed as part of a major modernisation programme, when what was originally the Grand Junction was merged with other canals to form the Grand Union.

Junction Canal from Braunston to the Thames was incorporated into a grouping of eight canals that were to form the Grand Union. A modernisation programme was put in place, which included rebuilding the 21 locks at Hatton and enlarging them to take 14-foot (4m) wide boats – or a pair of narrow boats side by side. The latter were the norm, for, by this date, motor boats had been introduced and the working pair was seen on the canal – the motor boat towing the unpowered butty behind it. Before modernisation, the locks had to be used twice to get both boats through.

Innovation did not end there. For the first time on the canals, a new material was used for construction – concrete – and new enclosed paddle gear was also introduced.

An even grander flight of locks carried the Kennet and Avon Canal up Caen Hill to Devizes. However, in the early 20th century the canal fell into disrepair and the last boat climbed the hill in 1948. And that would seem to have been the end of the story, but in the 1960s, restoration work on the canal began and by 1990 the locks were restored

to their former glory. They are a magnificent sight: 29 wide locks lift the canal 237 feet (72m) in 2 miles (3km). If arriving at the foot of Hatton is daunting, facing Caen Hill is even more so.

Keeping the flight supplied with water was always a problem, originally solved by building side ponds that acted like miniature reservoirs alongside each lock. Carved into the hillside, they add to the drama of the scene. Today, a pump-back system has been installed to ensure that there is always plenty of water in the canal above the locks.

Caen Hill is not the longest flight of locks in the country, however: that honour belongs to the flight of 30 (originally 31) at Tardebigge on the Worcester and Birmingham. They are built on a curved course, though, so one never sees more than a portion of the flight at any one time.

Perhaps the oddest flight on the system is The Bratch on the Staffs and Worcester. These locks are separated by very short pounds that at first sight seem wholly impractical. If one thinks of a boat coming down them, as it empties it would release a whole lockful of water, far more than the

BELOW: The Tardebigge flight is Britain's longest with 30 locks. It is rarely possible to see more than a few locks at a time when working the flight.

TOP: The five-lock staircase at Bingley lifts the Leeds and Liverpool Canal 60 feet (18m).

ABOVE: This photograph was taken early in the last century when the Bingley Five had been drained for maintenance and emphasises the grandeur of the scheme.

pound could hold; but a close look reveals side ponds terraced into the hillside. This seems an odd system as it would surely have been easier to run the locks straight into each other to create a watery staircase, which is exactly what James Brindley did when the canal was first built in the 1760s. The puzzle is why anyone would have wanted to change that – and it is a puzzle that so far remains unanswered.

As Brindley was working at developing a canal system in the Midlands, further north a major canal was under construction to link Leeds and Liverpool. Work began in 1770. At the eastern end, the canal charged up the Aire Valley in a series of ever greater leaps, starting with a double lock, then a three-lock staircase and culminating in the giant five-lock staircase at Bingley. Meeting a staircase for the first time can be bewildering. Going down is simple: water from the top lock empties into the one below and, once levels are equal, the gates can be opened and the process repeated. Climbing the staircase is, however, more complex. On entering a lock, nothing can be done unless the next lock above has been filled.

Bingley may leave holiday boaters scratching their heads, but no one can fail to be impressed by the five wide locks that carry the canal 60 feet

(18m) up the hillside. Bingley Five represents one of the great engineering works of the early period and the masonry work of the locks, made up of large stone blocks, is a credit to the craftsmanship of the men involved.

Work may have got off to a flying start on the Leeds and Liverpool, but the project was beset by problems, mainly financial, and was only opened throughout in 1816.

In 1803, work began on what was Britain's most ambitious canal project yet, the Caledonian. The two staircases here – a five-lock at Fort Augustus and an eight-lock forming Neptune's Staircase near Fort William were built to a massive scale.

For once, we are lucky enough to have an eyewitness account of just what was involved in constructing these immense staircases. The poet Robert Southey visited Fort Augustus with the chief engineer, Thomas Telford, in May 1819, when three of the locks had been completed. Unlike the workers labouring at Bingley, who had little in the way of mechanical aids to help them, the men at work here could make use of the latest technology. Because the bottom lock had to be excavated down to a depth below the riverbed, a steam engine had to be used to keep the water at bay, pumping it out at a rate of 8,000 gallons (36,370 litres) a

TOP: One of the pair of staircase locks at Foxton on the Leicester Arm of the Grand Union Canal.

ABOVE: The staircase at Fort Augustus links the artificial waterway, the Caledonian Canal, with Loch Ness at Fort Augustus.

ABOVE: The staircase of ship locks at Banavie on the Caledonian Canal, known as Neptune's Staircase, with Ben Nevis providing a dramatic background.

BELOW: The old Clyde Puffer, VIC 32, a small coal-fired steamer, passing through a lock on the Crinan Canal, built to save vessels from the long journey round the Mull of Kintyre.

minute. A steam dredger was at work widening the channel in front of the bottom lock. Rail tracks had been laid to remove spoil from the excavation, and iron lock gates had just arrived from Derbyshire. It must have been a scene of immense activity. It would be good to report that all this effort resulted in a highly successful waterway but sadly few ships ever needed to use it. However, today it is a popular route for holidaymakers and passing through the two staircases still makes one marvel at the workmanship and ingenuity of the engineers and their employees two centuries ago.

The Caledonian Canal was to remain the most ambitious of the country's canals until 1887, when work started on the Manchester Ship Canal. It dwarfed the Scottish waterway with locks theoretically able to take vessels up to 800 feet (244m) long and 65ft 6in (20m) wide. The technology available here was greater than anything Telford could have envisaged. Altogether, more than 100 excavators were used and some 200 cranes. Spoil was removed by wagons running on 223 miles (359km) of railway track worked by 173 steam locomotives. Yet, despite this, the canal still had to rely on some 16,000 navvies. It was the final fling for great canal projects in Britain.

Lock keepers and their houses

Locks need regular maintenance and that is the job of the lock keeper, but that is only part of the story. On river navigations, the lock keeper also has to be responsible for controlling the flow of water at the weirs, by opening and closing sluices to prevent sections either drying out or flooding, as conditions demand. On the canals, the lock keeper looks after a section of the canal, not just the locks, so is more accurately known as a 'lengthman'. In either case, the lock keeper needs a home beside the waterway – he needs a lock cottage.

There are no special requirements for these cottages: they are simple, small houses similar to those used by other working men and their families. They are the sort of dwellings any competent builder could produce in a plain, vernacular style. This could vary from one region to the next. On the Montgomery Canal, for example, the simple cottages have a distinctive Welsh vernacular flavour. White walls contrast with black window surrounds and edgings to walls. There are, however, notable exceptions. Thomas Telford had always had ambitions to work as an architect rather than a stonemason, the job for which he trained. Before he began working on canals, he had already designed two churches that were built in Shropshire. So, when he turned to engineering,

BELOW: An attractive lock cottage at Rushall on the Birmingham Canal Navigation system.

he also used his architectural skills in designing lock cottages. When he was appointed as the engineer working under the direction of the chief engineer, William Jessop, on the Ellesmere Canal, now known as the Llangollen, he showed off his skills. A key point was the three-lock staircase at Grindley Brook. The cottage is exceptionally grand, with a bay front and veranda. It is a reminder that the canals were built during the Georgian age and Telford's cottage has all the elegance associated with that era. On the Shropshire Union main line, he often added architectural detailing, such as setting windows into arched recesses, and on the Caledonian Canal he followed Scottish vernacular forms. There is a lovely little cottage at Kytra Lock, with the upper floor lit by dormer windows let into the roof. Telford, however, never strayed far from traditional forms. Others took more eccentric paths.

The cottages on the Thames and Severn are unique, a series of circular towers. These do not necessarily make for useful living spaces – circular rooms create problems. So why were they built in this manner? Circular buildings are not unusual at the western end of the canal, where Stroud was then the centre of a thriving wool industry. The fleeces had to be washed before being turned into yarn, and they were dried in wool stoves. One survivor can be seen at Woodchester, just south of Stroud. Now converted into a home, it is all but indistinguishable from lock cottages such as that at Chalford. Was the canal design a deliberate imitation of what were once familiar buildings in the region? It is possible.

Another unique design can be found on the Stratford-upon-Avon Canal. The canal had a troubled history. Work began in 1793 but by 1802 only the northern half had been completed and work only began again a decade later under William James, better known as a railway enthusiast than a canal engineer. The lock cottages are single-storey with barrel-vaulted roofs. Money was short and one theory is that because centring was available for constructing bridges, it could be used as the basis for roof construction. It is not a very convincing argument – James may simply have liked the design. They are very appealing and one is now available as a holiday let.

Locks and lock cottages are the features that punctuate canal journeys, bringing travel to a temporary stop. The pause provides an opportunity to enjoy the rich variety of styles that they offer.

PLACES TO VISIT

CAEN HILL LOCKS: Kennet and Avon, Devizes SN10 1QS.

HATTON LOCKS: Grand Union, Canal Lane, Hatton CV35 7JL.

NEPTUNE'S STAIRCASE LOCKS: Caledonian Canal, Great Glen Way, Banavie, Fort William PH33 7NG.

FOXTON STAIRCASE LOCKS: Grand Union, Leicester Arm, 4 miles west of Market Harborough LE16 7RA.

BINGLEY FIVE RISE LOCKS: Leeds and Liverpool, Beck Lane, Bingley BD16 2NA.

TOP: These barrel-vaulted cottages are unique to the Stratford-upon-Avon Canal. No one is altogether sure why the design was adopted.

BOTTOM: The Hanwell locks lift the Grand Union up from the Thames. The lock cottage is typically modest, though slightly unusual in having a hipped roof.

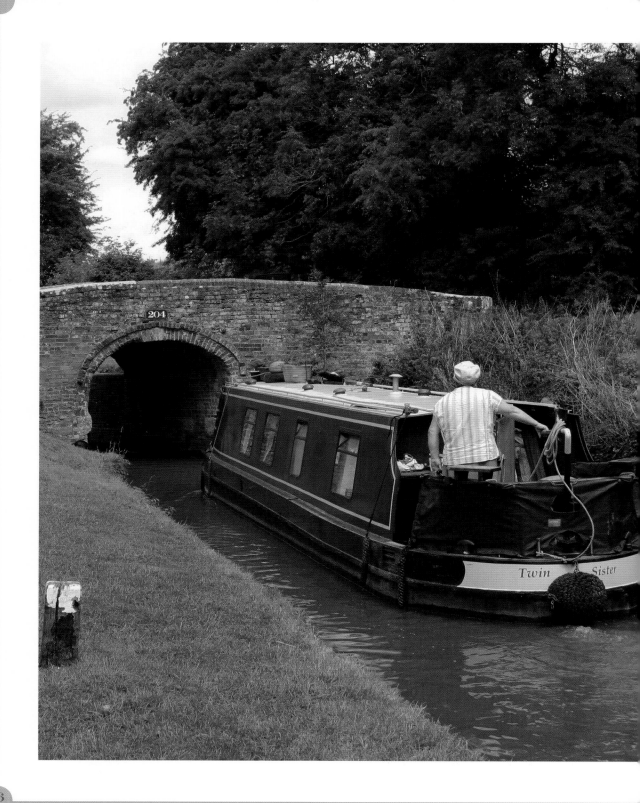

CHAPTER 3

BRIDGES

Canals cut across old divisions of the land, perhaps separating a farmer from his fields or slicing through a country lane. The company would purchase the land needed for the waterway but were under a legal obligation to provide appropriate access to land on either side of the cut. They had to build bridges. The design we all associate with canals is the hump-backed bridge, which appears to be a very simple structure, but there is far more to it than might appear. For a start, there is the choice of materials to be used in construction.

Brick and stone

One of the main reasons for building canals in the first place was the wretched state of so many of the country's roads, which made it uneconomical to bring materials from far away. So, where stone was available, the company would purchase it from a local quarry or even open up a quarry of their own. Elsewhere they would use brick. The modern brick is mainly mass produced, turning out identical products, each brick being precisely the same shape, size and colour as the next. This was not the case in the 18th century. Every brick would have been made by hand in a wooden mould, before being dried in the open air and fired in a kiln. The amount of heat reaching the bricks depended on its place in the complex stacking arrangement. As a result, there were always irregularities and bricks from the same firing could differ markedly in colour and texture. The result is that where a modern brick building may present a rather boring uniformity to the world, the bricks in even the most ordinary canal bridge have a richness and variety that can be a visual delight, and that richness only develops with age.

Stone bridges also mature gracefully, but here the differences depend on the type of stone available locally, so that the honey-coloured limestone found on the Kennet and Avon gives the structure a totally different appearance to that given to the Pennine canals by the dark gritstone of the region. Variations can also be found in the ways the stone is treated: the face can be dressed to present a smooth, flat surface to the world or left rough-hewn. But whether stone or brick, all the structures have one thing in common: they all reflect the geology and nature of their own specific region. They fit in and seem comfortably at home in the landscape.

LEFT: A typical hump-backed canal bridge, built of mellow brick, at the tail of a lock on the Oxford Canal.

Bridge design

Their design is visually attractive but is dictated by practical necessities. The company never wanted to spend more money than absolutely necessary. The bridge had merely to span the water and the towpath and provide sufficient headroom for the boat and the horse that pulled it to pass underneath, and no more. The arch above the water and towpath would be built on wooden centring, but considerable skill was required from the bricklayer or mason as the curve of the arch would be of a rather shorter radius than that of the parapet. In the case of brick bridges, the inside of the arch and the parapet would be protected by stone. The greatest wear came from the tow rope

LEFT: A metal bridge guard sculpted by decades of friction from tow ropes.

BELOW: Canal engineers were as frugal as possible: the bridge at Alrewas only has space for one boat to pass at a time.

as the horse passed under the bridge, which over the years would result in deep grooves cut into even the hardest stone. Extra protection was often supplied by fixing iron plates to the inside of the arch but even these could not resist the relentless friction of the passing trade. Over time, they too were sculpted into fantastic shapes.

A bridge on the Regent's Canal as it passes Regent's Park might baffle those who don't know the story. The iron pillars that support the bridge on the towpath side show the usual marks of wear, but on the wrong side, as though the horses have been dragging boats along the path instead of the water. The answer lies in a fatal accident of 1874 when a boat loaded with gunpowder blew up, demolishing the bridge. It was rebuilt and, in the process, the supports were reversed. Ever since, it has been popularly known as 'Blow-up Bridge'.

One way to minimise the use of material was to situate the bridge at the tail of a lock. As the horse didn't go through the lock, there was no need for a towpath under the bridge. There are many examples around the country, but a favourite is at King's lock, Tattershall on the Trent and Mersey, where all the elements meet to perfection: the narrow lock in a rural setting, the neat bridge and the lock cottage in a simple vernacular style. Sometimes, however, more extreme measures were called for. The bridge over the deep cutting at East Marton on the Leeds and Liverpool had to be tall, and the engineer played safe by using a double arch, one above the other, for strength. Even more dramatic are the bridges crossing the deep cuts on the Shropshire Union, where the abutments climb from canal level to the top of the cutting. The shape of the arch has led them to be known as 'rocket' bridges. Some bridges needed to be more elaborate than normal.

BELOW: Blow-up Bridge on the Regent's Canal owes its name to a 19th-century disaster when a vessel loaded with gunpowder exploded beneath it. The pieces were rebuilt as before but with the supporting pillars reversed.

RIGHT: This scene near Fradley typifies the charm of the canals with lock, attractive lock cottage and a neat brick bridge.

BELOW: A rare sight on the canals these days: a working narrow boat approaching the bridge at King's Lock on the Trent and Mersey. This is a popular spot, not least because of the presence of a lock-side pub.

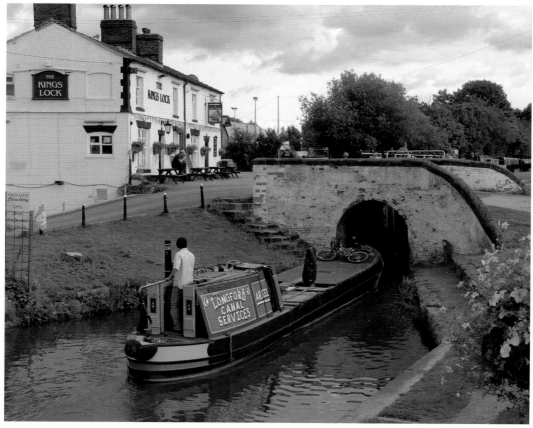

The bridge and lock at Somerton: the cottage has a little window in the gable end to provide the lock keeper with a view down the canal.

LEFT: The Shropshire Union Canal is noted for its deep cuttings. This one at Grub Street is spanned by a typically tall bridge, popularly known as a rocket bridge from the shape of the opening.

ABOVE: This double-arched bridge at East Marton on the Leeds and Liverpool Canal is built of stone. Like other bridges on this canal, the navigation centre of the opening is marked in white, to the left of the crown of the arch.

Canal junctions, where a second canal – often a branch canal – meets the main line, present a specific problem. The main line towpath has to be carried over the branch line, but in order to keep the towline at a reasonable angle, so it is not trying to haul the bows into the air, the approach has to be along a gently sloping ramp. So, as a result, the bridge has more sinuous curves than the normal bridge, and an elegant outline. There are several notable examples, but just picking two from opposite ends of the country: Bull's Bridge, where the Paddington Arm meets the main line of the Grand Union, and Barbridge, the meeting point of the Shropshire Union and the Middlewich Branch.

TOP RIGHT: Great Haywood Junction is the meeting point for the Staffs and Worcester and Trent and Mersey canals, and is crossed by this typically elegant brick bridge.

BOTTOM RIGHT: One of the most attractive of junction bridges is at Barbridge, where the Middlewich Branch joins the Shropshire Union main line.

BELOW: Bull's Bridge Junction marks the point where the main line of the Grand Union Canal carries on down to the Thames and the Paddington Arm turns off to the left. The bridge had to be extended beyond the usual limits so that horses on the main line can cross the bridge on a gentle slope.

Turnover bridges are needed when the towpath changes from one side of the canal to the other. The most sophisticated solution to the problem of getting the horse across without having to unharness it can be seen in the magnificent bridges of the Macclesfield Canal.

A second difficulty occurs when, for some reason or other, it is necessary to move the towpath from one side of the canal to the other. Obviously, the horse can't simply walk over a bridge dragging the boat behind it. Unhitching the horse and reattaching it on the other side is time-consuming, so what is required is a special turnover bridge. The simplest version has a long approach ramp to take the horse on to the bridge and then, on the other side, a second ramp parallel to the first. Once back on the towpath, the horse can be turned to walk back under the bridge. A far more elegant solution, however, was found on the Macclesfield Canal. Here, the stone turnover bridges are built as a spiral, with the path curling back under itself. They are often known as 'snake bridges', but in many ways they are more like the spirals of a snail shell. They are undoubtedly the most intriguing and attractive bridges on the whole system.

A very special difficulty appeared when canal and road met at an angle that is not a right angle. Stones cannot be laid in courses parallel to the ground, but instead have to be at an angle, which requires considerable skill on the part of the mason in dressing the individual stones to fit the pattern. There is a fine example on the Lancaster Canal. Some authorities suggest that the skew bridge was developed by railway engineers – but the canals got there first.

It was not just engineering necessities that demanded a change from the standard pattern. Sometimes the canal passed through or close to the estate of some influential person. This happened when the Grand Junction reached the grounds of the Earls of Essex at what is now Cassiobury Park. Gothic was then the rage and their lordships demanded a Gothic bridge, with a pointed arch instead of the familiar semicircular arch. They also managed to have a nearby lock cottage built in a similar style.

BELOW: Although most bridges are strictly functional, where the canal passed through or close to the estate of some grandee, the company were obliged to provide something special. This example is at Grove Park on the Grand Union.

Movable bridges

That so many old brick and stone bridges can still be seen is a tribute to their durability, but they were expensive to construct. A common problem faced many canal companies – problems far from unknown on contemporary major engineering works. Estimates were prepared when the Act of Parliament was being sought, setting out in detail exactly what it would cost to complete the work, and the money was then raised by selling shares. All too often those estimates proved wildly inaccurate. As an indignant shareholder wrote, the Kennet and Avon had been estimated to cost £400,000 and that had all been spent and it looked as if the final cost would be over a million. In these circumstances, companies looked for savings, and one area where costs could be cut was to replace expensive fixed bridges by cheaper movable versions. These would require expensive maintenance in the long term and would cause delays to boats but they met the immediate need for economy.

There are two basic ways of building these structures: have the bridge platform either swing horizontally or rise vertically. Vertical lift bridges can be simple or quite complex. The most basic consist of just a platform across the water and a long, angled beam to act as a lever – rather like a lock gate and balance beam set on the side. This is comparatively crude and there is an obvious problem in that, with use, the strains on the joint between the beam and the platform will lead to weakness, with the far end of the platform being

LEFT: Lift bridges were cheaper to construct than permanent structures: this example on the Oxford Canal is as basic as it can be.

LEFT: The lift bridges on the Llangollen Canal are quite sophisticated: the overhead beams provide support for the bridge platform and prevent it drooping over time.

Avenue Bridge on the Shropshire Union: the curved abutments and balustrade have converted a plain bridge into one appropriate for carrying the driveway to a gentleman's mansion.

unsupported and liable to sag. Lift bridges of this type can be seen on the Oxford Canal, for example. The problem of stresses can be overcome by having a more complex arrangement, the type of bridge often seen in early paintings of Dutch canals. Here, supporting posts, like elongated goalposts, act as the pivot for a pair of beams, connected at both ends. At one end, chains lead down to the end of the platform furthest from the support. A chain at the opposite end, suspended from the superstructure, allows the beam on the towpath side to be pulled down, raising the platform. This is mechanically a far better arrangement. There is, however, a snag. It only works when the chain on the towpath side is actually present. The author still remembers meeting one of these bridges on the canal near Llangollen with no chain and having to heave up the platform by hand, allowing just enough space for the boat to squeeze through.

LEFT: The Llanthony lift bridge at the entrance to the Gloucester and Sharpness Canal at Gloucester Docks was built in 1972, the third to be built on the site.

BELOW: The modern lift bridge on the Sheffield and South Yorkshire Navigation replaced an earlier swing bridge. It is a massive structure and needed to be, as it carried heavy traffic to the nearby Thorpe Marsh power station.

The swing bridge is more complicated to construct. As with the lift bridge, the platform is moved by means of a beam acting as a long lever. At the end, opposite the towpath, a semicircular opening in the wall allows for the movement and the end of the platform rests on rollers. There is generally some sort of overhead system of stays to support the platform and prevent it sagging under its own weight. Bridges such as these work well, but only if well maintained: if not, they can cause an immense amount of trouble. Whichever type is used, they are an inconvenience. Travellers on the Leeds and Liverpool Canal might think that once they have climbed the Bingley Five they have in front of them the long pound, 14 miles (22km) of lock-free travel and the prospect of an easy life, but the route is peppered by swing bridges to interrupt the journey. The canal is, however, notable for its simple pedestrian bridges at locks. These consist

BELOW: Apart from the Llanthony lift bridge, all the bridges on the Gloucester and Sharpness Canal are swing bridges.

of single baulks of timber, with guard rails set at an angle – an economic use of material based on the fact that we are rather broader in the midriff area than we are at our feet.

One other but much rarer form of movable bridge was built, in which the whole platform was raised vertically, instead of being tilted upwards. An example can be seen at the Black Country Living Museum in Dudley. It originally stood at the Lloyds Proving House at Tipton by the transhipment dock,

ABOVE: The swing bridge is the alternative to the lift bridge: this simple example is on the Leeds and Liverpool Canal.

where cargoes were exchanged between rail and canal. The weight of the platform is balanced by heavy weights suspended from chains. As a result, the deck can be raised using a simple hand winch. One of the very few working bridges of this type is to be found on the Huddersfield Broad Canal.

Iron bridges

The movable bridges discussed so far were chosen by the engineers as cheap alternatives, but when it came to ship canals they were essential: no one wanted to build bridges high enough for a tall-masted ship to pass underneath. The two major works of the canal-building period were the Gloucester and Berkeley – now the Gloucester and Sharpness – and Caledonian ship canals, both featuring swing bridges. Because of the width of the canal, the Caledonian bridges come in two halves which, before mechanisation, meant that the bridge keeper had to boat across to the opposite bank once one half had been swung. Because the bridge keepers had to be constantly on duty, they needed to be housed next to their bridges. The Caledonian houses are similar to the lock cottages, but the Gloucestershire versions are very unusual. In general, such buildings are quite plain, but these have architectural pretensions, fronted by neoclassical porticos. The additions might have looked at home fronting some grand Georgian house, but seem out of scale with these modest cottages. The other feature that distinguishes the bridges is the use of iron instead of timber, as this was a material that was not available at the start of the canal age.

At the start of the 18th century, Abraham Darby of Coalbrookdale discovered a way of smelting iron ore using coke. Where the older furnaces had used charcoal as a fuel and produced malleable wrought iron, the new system produced cast iron and in 1779 the material was used for the world's first iron bridge, which spanned the River Severn close to the Darby works – and gave its name to the riverside town of Ironbridge. It was a slightly curious affair, with the cast iron sections being treated like timber, joined together with mortice and dovetail joints. But the advantages of this new construction method were immediately obvious and soon found a place in the canal world.

BELOW: The smooth curve of the iron bridge at Hawkesbury Junction, spanning the entrance to the Coventry Canal.

An important feature of the end of the 18th century was the improvement of the connections between the Midlands and London. The Grand Junction Canal linked to Birmingham via other waterways, including the wayward northern section of the Oxford. It was decided to rebuild the latter on a much straighter line. The other wandering waterway was Brindley's original Birmingham Canal. Thomas Telford was given the task of building a new Birmingham main line. All this work involved providing a lot of new bridges. The new Birmingham main line, for example, cut through the line of the old canal, leaving, as mentioned earlier, a series of loops. Each loop had to be bridged twice for the main line towpath.

The original iron bridge over the Severn was a one-off, but the advantage of cast iron is that once a pattern has been made, it can be used to reproduce that particular piece over and over again. This proved invaluable. Canals are generally built to a uniform width, so the same bridge design can be employed at any place along the line. The Horseley ironworks were set up on the Horseley Branch of the Birmingham Canal, with new furnaces built in 1808 and 1809. The company set about manufacturing standard bridges. The bridges were

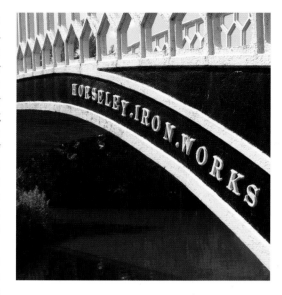

ABOVE: By the end of the 19th century, cast iron was beginning to replace brick and stone for bridges, and the most famous manufacturers were the Horseley ironworks at Tipton.

RIGHT: The split bridge over a lock on the Stratford Canal allows the tow rope to be passed through. It is not strictly speaking split at all, but two cantilevered platforms almost meeting in the middle.

BELOW: A trio of Horseley bridges at Windmill End.

One of the most elegant iron bridges can be seen at the river end of the Duke's Cut on the Oxford Canal.

cast in sections consisting of two flat arches, with integral handrails, joined together by a central locking plate. The decks were created from smaller iron plates, bolted together. The arches spring from simple abutments of stone or brick.

Iron could also be used in ways that older materials could not. Turnover bridges were discussed earlier, and the obvious fact that boats couldn't simply be dragged over the top. But with iron, the tow rope could actually pass though the bridge. This can be seen at locks on the Stratford Canal with what are generally called split bridges. In fact, what you have are two cantilevered platforms that don't quite meet, leaving a gap for the rope. An ingenious solution to an old problem.

Other far grander iron bridges were constructed over the years, one of the best examples of which was also part of the Birmingham improvement scheme overseen by Telford. Part of the work involved creating a deep cutting at Smethwick that sliced across the line of Galton Street. A bridge

was needed, and an elegant iron structure was built arcing over the cutting in a single 151-foot (46m) span. Sadly, the bridge failed to meet the needs of modern traffic, so a new, lower bridge was constructed and the canal consigned to a tunnel through its embankment. The grand visual effect was lost.

Iron also lends itself well to decorative effects. The Kennet and Avon Canal passes through fashionable Sydney Gardens in Bath, where Georgian ladies and gentlemen paraded and chatted. A common, plain bridge was unthinkable in such a setting, but a refined iron bridge became an asset rather than an eyesore.

RIGHT: Telford's magnificent Galton Bridge strides majestically over the Birmingham Canal.

BELOW: The Kennet and Avon passes through the fashionable Sydney Gardens in Bath, and a suitably ornate bridge was provided.

Bridge construction did not end after canal building came to an end, but this book is primarily concerned with the work of the original canal engineers. However, new additions have had an impact, producing spectacular structures and surprises. Most railways simply soared high over the canal, as if demonstrating their superiority to what then seemed already an antiquated form of transport, but there are some curiosities. The railway crosses the Stainforth and Keadby Canal in the flat land bordering the Trent. The bridge passes just a few feet above the water but has been designed to slide to one side to allow boats to pass. The problem for those coming this way by water is that the line is busy and they must wait patiently for a gap in the traffic.

The coming of the motorways in the 20th century profoundly affected some parts of the system and nowhere more so than round Birmingham. At one point, one of the massive concrete pillars holding the M3 sits right in the centre of the Birmingham Canal, while the Birmingham and Fazeley runs directly under the complex at Spaghetti Junction. And the modern world has added some bridges that truly enhance the scene, none more so than the sculptural footbridge at Castlefield Basin in Manchester. Yet it is the old bridges that set the character of our canals, and one never travels the waterways without seeing something new. For example, while travelling the Shropshire Union with my old friend Peter White, he spotted a novel use of a bridge. Canals sometimes need to be drained for maintenance, which involves isolating a section using stop planks as temporary dams. Here, an arched recess had been cut into the abutment to keep the planks tucked away out of the rain. It was a small detail, but discovering that the waterways are full of such little quirks keeps one coming back time and time again.

LEFT: The M6 overshadows the Birmingham and Fazeley Canal at Spaghetti Junction: powerful and utilitarian, but hardly elegant.

BRIDGE NUMBERS

It is easy to underestimate the immense amount of work needed to supply bridges across canals. For example, the Trent and Mersey has a total of 213 bridges on its 93-mile (150km) length. Size that up for the whole network and you can estimate that around 5,000 bridges were built. Each one is numbered on the individual canal, originally with painted numerals, but later with distinctive cast iron plates.

PLACES TO VISIT

GALTON BRIDGE, BIRMINGHAM CANAL, Roebuck Lane, Smethwick, B66 1BY.

'SNAKE' TURNOVER BRIDGE, Macclesfield Canal, Marple Junction, Marple SK6 6BN.

ORNAMENTAL BRIDGE, Grand Union Canal, Cassiobury Park, Watford WD18 7LG.

HORSELEY IRON BRIDGE, Hawkesbury Junction, Longford, Coventry CV6 6DF.

LIFT BRIDGE, Huddersfield Broad Canal, Turnbridge Road, Turnbridge HD1 6AG.

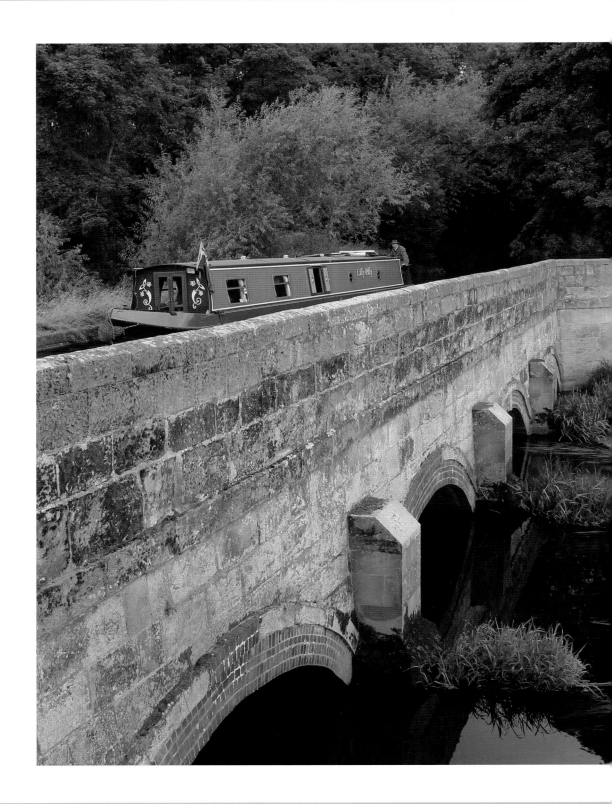

CHAPTER 4

AQUEDUCTS

Canal aqueducts were not new when James Brindley began work on the Bridgewater Canal, but they were completely unknown in Britain. The Duke of Bridgewater himself would almost certainly have seen one on the Canal du Midi in southern France, which he visited when he went on that essential trip for all young aristocrats, The Grand Tour. Not that he had aqueducts in mind when he first planned for a canal to take coal from his mines at Worsley into the heart of Manchester: he had hoped to make a short cutting to join the navigable River Irwell. But the river authorities turned him down, so the bold decision was taken: if the canal could not join the river then it would soar above it at Barton.

Brindley's aqueducts

In many ways, the construction of an aqueduct is not very different from that of a bridge, apart from the fact that instead of a roadway it carries a trough full of water. But this difference is important. Earth had been piled on top of the basic bridge structure and it was into this earth that the channel was cut. The trough then had to be made watertight, which in the case of the Barton aqueduct meant lining it with puddled clay, the mixture that was used to line canals. It therefore carried a considerable weight, and the finished main structure was built up of massive stone blocks. The river itself was crossed by two segmented arches, with a third semicircular arch on the land. It could not be called a handsome structure. There are no decorative details, though

LEFT: Brindley's aqueduct on the Staffs and Worcester Canal has none of the drama of his Barton aqueduct, as it only has to cross the unnavigable River Sow and could be built on low arches.

the piers that sit in the river have pointed cutwaters to smooth the flow of water. Every effort was made to ensure that it was solid, but in the event the engineers had been too cautious. Brindley had insisted on such a depth of puddled clay in the trough that the stonework began to show signs of splitting once the water was run in. It had to be rapidly drained, and a great deal of the puddle removed. When that was done, there was no sign of any leaks and the stonework was stabilised.

The Barton aqueduct was considered a wonder when it opened in 1761, and it became a tourist attraction. People came to marvel at the sight of a boat on the canal passing high above the barges on the river. What was even more impressive for those who understood such things was the ease with which boats could pass up and down the canal, while boats coming upstream against the current on the Irwell required a far greater effort. It made Brindley famous, but now historians believe that most of the planning was down to the Duke's agent, John Gilbert. Certainly, Brindley never built anything on this scale again, but then he never needed to do so. His later aqueducts were over unnavigable rivers, so there was no need to provide space for boats to pass underneath. A typical example is the one that takes the Staffs and Worcester Canal across the River Sow. It is carried on four segmented masonry arches, lined with brick. The actual masonry work consists of large, squared stone blocks of irregular size, with a string course and parapet above the arches. It is a practical structure that has stood the test of time, but it can hardly be described as a thing of grace and beauty.

Rennie's aqueducts

There was a lull in canal building in the 1770s and 80s but the early 1790s became known as the years of canal mania, with a rush of new and important canals being constructed, and it is in this period that we find some of the grandest and most elegant aqueducts being constructed. The finest examples in terms of architectural style are those designed by John Rennie, the chief engineer for the Kennet and Avon Canal. He designed the canal

so that as it left the River Avon in Bath, it climbed through a flight of locks to a point at the edge of the valley, well above the river, which meant he was able to continue all the way to Bradford on Avon as a lock-free pound for 10 miles (16km). He did, however, have a problem. At first the canal ran to the north of the river, but then rising ground made it necessary to cross to the opposite side to keep the level – and further on, the reverse situation arose and it crossed back again. So, he needed to provide two aqueducts, and it is one nearer Bath that is the chief glory of the canal.

The Dundas aqueduct, named after the canal company's chairman, Lord Dundas, could be thought of as the engineer's tribute to the elegance of Bath. It is built from the same oolitic limestone, so closely associated with the city that it is popularly known as Bath stone. There was a source of stone near at hand at Bathampton, so there was no problem with supply. The stone has a very special quality, notably a rich honey colour,

BELOW: An 18th-century illustration of the original Barton aqueduct. Tourists came to marvel at the sight of boats on the Bridgewater Canal passing over boats on the River Irwell.

ABOVE: The elegant Dundas aqueduct
carries the Kennet and Avon Canal over the
River Avon near Bath.

that can seem almost buttery on a fine, sunny day – and it is admirably suited to the neoclassical style fashionable in Bath. Because we think of canals in an industrial setting, it is easy to forget that the age in which they were built was also the age of the great Georgian architects. Rennie was to provide his own architectural embellishments. The Avon itself is crossed by a single semicircular arch, with relieving arches on the land to either side. Pilasters decorate the piers between the arches, above which is a deep dentil cornice. The whole structure is topped by a balustrade, with the individual supports elegantly curved. As with all the best Georgian architecture, the effect is enhanced by the careful attention to proportion and detail. The other aqueduct, at Avoncliff, is notably less attractive. It has none of the architectural detailing of Dundas and was built from the local ragstone, which has not worn well and as a result there has been a lot of rough patching to the stonework over the years. It is not, however, without its interest as it is a reminder that, like other canals, the Kennet and Avon was built to serve industry. There is a pair of watermills, one a woollen mill and the other a flock mill, down by the river, and originally a tramway – an early horse-drawn railway – ran along

ABOVE: The elegant Dundas aqueduct carries the Kennet and Avon Canal over the River Avon near Bath.

the towpath and over the aqueduct, which explains the width of the towpath.

Rennie's other great work was the aqueduct that carries the Lancaster Canal over the River Lune, just outside Lancaster. This is a massive structure, 664 feet (202m) long, crossing the river on five semicircular arches at a height of 61 feet (19m). It uses a similar classical language to that employed at Dundas, but the effect is very different. Lancaster is a northern working city and was then a busy port, not a spa attracting the wealthy and fashionable. Here, the local stone is tough millstone grit, so instead of the smooth ashlar of Dundas, the blocks on the Lune aqueduct are left uncut, presenting a rough, uneven face to the world, known appropriately in architectural terms as rusticated. This is an aqueduct that we actually know a great deal about, as detailed records have survived from the construction period, giving us an insight into what was involved in creating such a grand structure.

Building the Lune aqueduct

The first stage was to build coffer dams on the riverbed. These were constructed by driving in piles to create an area that could be pumped dry by means of a steam engine. Once that was completed, workers could be lowered into the space to begin constructing the foundations for the piers. Pile-driving was arduous work. Sawyers were involved to cut the massive timber posts, then the workmen had to sink them into the riverbed, down to a solid base. This was manual work, and one report recorded a workman losing three fingers, being caught under the pile-driver. Once the dam was completed, it had to be constantly pumped dry – an occupation that had an unexpected drawback as the 'steam engine man' was something of a drunkard who 'always had the can to his head'. Work inside the dams was unpleasant: they were never completely watertight, so the men were constantly working in damp, cloying clay, and the company minutes recorded that extra beer was handed out to keep them contented. It was a scene of great activity: carts were constantly going to and fro, bringing stone from the nearest quarry. Carpenters were employed creating the centrings on which the arches could be built and the labourers were busy, not just on the aqueduct itself but also in preparing the approaches. In the summer of 1794, when work had begun on the second pier, there were 127 navvies, 22 carpenters and 14 sawyers at work. When it was completed in 1797 it had cost the company £48,321, roughly £5.5 million at today's prices.

Outram's innovation

The Peak Forest Canal was the work of Benjamin Outram, an engineer better known for designing tramways. He was a partner in the very successful Butterley ironworks, but it seems that the idea of using iron as a building material did not occur to him when it came to constructing an aqueduct

BELOW: John Rennie's aqueduct taking the Lancaster Canal over the River Lune is in the same classical idiom as Dundas, but uses rough-hewn instead of dressed stone facings.

across the River Goyt. He may have been influenced by the fact that there was plenty of good building stone in the region, so there was no need to try a new material. But he did, however, make use of one innovation. William Edwards of Pontypridd had designed a bridge across the River Taff with a single 140-foot (45m) wide arch. He found it very difficult to stabilise it, and eventually realised that the problem was caused by the sheer weight of masonry in the spandrels, the area to the side of the arches. To reduce the weight, he left a cylindrical hole in the spandrels, which solved the problem without weakening the structure. Outram, who had been busy with tramways in South Wales, knew about the bridge and adopted the device of pierced spandrels for his aqueduct. This canal remained derelict for several years and its reopening has given boaters the opportunity to cross and admire this fine structure, the Marple aqueduct, in an attractive setting.

BELOW: The long flight of locks that takes the Peak Forest Canal down from Marple ends in the fine aqueduct across the River Goyt.

Iron aqueducts

Another restoration scheme has also brought magnificent aqueducts back to life, but this time in Scotland. The Edinburgh and Glasgow Union Canal was quite a latecomer: work only started in 1817. The chief engineer was Hugh Baird. Despite its name, it didn't actually get to Glasgow but joined the Forth and Clyde Canal at Falkirk. There were three large aqueducts on the line, of which the most interesting is the one that carries the canal high above the wooded valley of the River Almond. With a total length of 420 feet (128m) and a height above the river of 76 feet (23m), it is an imposing structure. Baird originally planned to carry the aqueduct on a single arch, with embankments at either end to bring the canal to the right level. He was persuaded to change his mind by Thomas Telford, and eventually there were four arches, two of them over the river. It differed from the aqueducts described so far in that the trough was not lined with puddled clay but instead had a trough constructed from cast iron. To find out how iron came to be used in canal aqueducts, we need to go back again to the 1790s.

The Almond aqueduct is one of the most imposing features on the Edinburgh and Glasgow Union Canal.

The Ellesmere Canal was not the most important link in the growing network, and the chief engineer, William Jessop, was a busy man, with many projects to oversee, including the Grand Junction, the canal that would link London to Birmingham and the north. He needed a man on the ground, a resident engineer, to make sure his plans were correctly carried out. The job went to Thomas Telford, then County Surveyor for Shropshire but with no previous experience of canal work. There was one major problem to overcome: how to cross the wide, deep valley of the River Dee near Llangollen. But before any decision on that could be reached, Telford was called away in 1795 to finish work on another waterway, the Shrewsbury Canal. This had been started under the leadership of Josiah Clowes, and he had designed an aqueduct to cross the River Tern at Longdon. This was a modest affair as the river was not navigable, so it was an easy matter to cross it with a low masonry structure. Visit the site today and you can still see the stone abutments begun under Clowes. But before it was finished, two things happened: a flood washed away the workings and Clowes died. The obvious thing was simply to carry on where Clowes had left off, but Telford was familiar, from his time as County Surveyor, with several of the leading ironmasters of the area. One of these was

William Reynolds, a promoter of the canal. He was keen to find new uses for his metal and suggested to Telford that the gap should now be filled by an iron trough, supported on iron pillars. It is a very basic structure, with the towpath carried on the outside of the trough. The triangular supports are bedded in stone foundations. It is an entirely utilitarian affair, but of unique importance, and has been preserved even though the canal itself has long since fallen into disuse. The advantages of using iron are at once obvious: it is far lighter than masonry and can be made watertight without the need to puddle the inside of the trough. There is little doubt that Reynolds and Telford saw this primarily as a way of testing a new idea rather than as an essential solution to a problem in crossing the Tern. It was soon to lead to greater things.

Telford returned to the Ellesmere Canal convinced he now had the answer to that troublesome crossing of the Dee valley – an iron trough aqueduct. His idea was accepted and the result was the magnificent Pontcysyllte, now a World Heritage site. There has been controversy over the years as to who should take the credit for it. For a long time, it was simply spoken of as Telford's masterpiece, but Charles Hadfield, the doyen of canal historians, was adamant that the main credit should go to Jessop. His argument was simple:

RIGHT: Telford's aqueduct at Longdon-upon-Tern was his first experiment with an iron trough. The abutments of the original stone aqueduct can be seen in the foreground.

Jessop was the chief engineer, it was ultimately his decision and his responsibility. He and I argued very amicably about this one over many years, and although we never reached complete agreement, we eventually decided that both deserved to be honoured. It was the innovation of Reynolds and Telford at Longdon that had opened the way but, as Charles pointed out, it was Jessop's decision. What remains absolutely indisputable is that this is one of Britain's engineering triumphs.

The scale of Pontcysyllte alone is impressive enough, at 1,007 feet (307m) long and standing 121 feet (37m) above the River Dee. The trough is carried on 18 stone piers, which are not quite what they seem. The masonry is solid up to a height of 70 feet (21m), above which they are hollow, braced with cross walls. The trough itself differs from Longdon in that this time the towpath is on the inside, suspended over the water on brackets. This has an obvious advantage in allowing a greater width of water so that even though the width available to the boat is not very great, there is less resistance to movement. With such a great length, the trough had to be made up of individual plates, the size of which was determined by the available casting technology of the furnaces at the nearby Plas Kynaston ironworks. The plates were designed in a variety of different shapes, with sloping sides: it

is easier to make a watertight joint when they meet at an angle than if they simply abut each other. There are iron supports also created out of wedge-shaped sections running between the supporting pillars. Crossing the aqueduct is an interesting experience. The horse walking the towpath had railings on the side to prevent a fall, but for the steerer in the stern, the side of the boat inevitably runs right up against the edge of the trough. It is the nearest one can get to flying in a narrow boat.

ABOVE: Following the success of the aqueduct over the River Tern, Telford went on to design his masterpiece, Pontcysyllte, seen in this aerial view striding high over the Dee valley.

LEFT: A boat in the iron trough of Pontcysyllte, with walkers on the cantilevered towpath.

The other aqueduct on the canal, at Chirk, appears at first sight to be a conventional masonry structure, but it has one novel feature. The trough is not lined with clay, but with iron plates bolted together and bonded into the masonry. It is, in effect, a hybrid, both a masonry and an iron trough aqueduct. It is a rarity, but not the only example. The Union Canal versions have already been mentioned and there is another at Nynehead in Somerset on the Grand Western Canal. Little of the canal now remains, but the aqueduct itself has survived in remarkably good condition.

The success of Pontcysyllte resulted in other engineers turning away from masonry to iron, including Jessop, who used it for his Grand Junction Canal aqueduct across the Great Ouse at Wolverton. Another engineer who turned to iron was William James, who was engineer for the southern section of the Stratford Canal. James was obviously a man with an eye for the latest thing, for he was soon to turn from canals to become a passionate advocate for railways. There are three aqueducts, of which the grandest is at Edstone.

ABOVE: Edstone aqueduct on the Stratford Canal has the towpath outside the iron trough.

It is a practical rather than an elegant structure, with a very basic construction. A row of piers, rather like overgrown children's building blocks, are lined up and the trough sits on top of them. Like Longdon, it has the towpath set outside the trough. It is not very high, but at 475 feet (145m) long it has the distinction of being the longest iron aqueduct in England. There was one other important aqueduct that is actually contemporary with Longdon, and was built by Benjamin Outram to carry the Derby Canal over the River Derwent. When the canal was closed the aqueduct was removed, but it was recognised as historically important, so all the iron parts were carefully labelled and stored by the local council with the possibility of eventual reconstruction. Sadly, not everyone recognised its importance and one enthusiastic official decided to swell the council's coffers by selling it off for scrap.

It would seem that the iron aqueducts could never enjoy the elaborate architectural treatment that was possible with stone, but Telford had other ideas. He was engineer for the Birmingham and Liverpool Junction Canal, which was later to join others to form the Shropshire Union, the name by which it is usually known today. Just beyond Brewood the canal crosses the A5, which lies on the route of Roman Watling Street. Telford had a great admiration for the Romans: while he was County Surveyor for Shropshire, he had been involved in the excavation of the Roman remains at Wroxeter. The juxtaposition was irresistible. The aqueduct itself is a simple affair of bolted iron plates, but it was embellished to a high degree. Ornate iron railings stand at either side, and decorative panels face the outside of the trough, in the centre of which Telford had his own name cast with the date 1832, and just to make sure no one missed it, he added tall circular stone pillars at both ends of the trough. It was, perhaps, something of a vanity project, but he was nearing the end of a long and successful career and can easily be forgiven.

The other Telford project came out of another important undertaking. As mentioned earlier, he was employed to create a new Birmingham main line that would slice through the looping curves of the old, and at one point he had to provide an aqueduct at Smethwick that would carry a short branch canal. Work took place at the end of the 1820s, a period when neoclassicism was beginning to lose favour and Gothic was on the ascendancy. Telford had always had architectural ambitions, and his new Engine Arm aqueduct was embellished with rows of pointed arches topped by trefoil decoration. It is the sort of effect one expects to find in Victorian architecture, not in the Georgian era.

BELOW: When Telford built the Stretton aqueduct over what is now the A5, he added pillars and an inscription to make sure road travellers noticed it.

The Engine Arm aqueduct over the Birmingham Canal reflects changing tastes as the 18th century gave way to the 19th: instead of classical features, it is decorated with pointed Gothic arches.

'Modern' aqueducts

By the 1830s, canal construction was drawing to a close and investors were putting their money instead into the burgeoning railway system. However, there was to be one major development when work began in 1887 on the Manchester Ship Canal. It was to swallow up the old Irwell Navigation, but to allow the new, big ships to pass, the old Barton aqueduct had to go. In its place, a new swing aqueduct was built. The trough dwarfs anything seen before – 18 feet (5.5m) wide and mounted on iron girders each 235 feet (72m) long. The whole structure is carried on iron rollers mounted on a central pier, and the trough is moved by hydraulic machinery. When movement is needed, the two ends of the trough are closed off by gates held watertight by wooden wedges. It is seldom used these days, but I was fortunate enough to see it in action when travelling on the Bridgewater Canal some years ago. The progress was slow and stately and there did not seem to be so much as a drop of water being lost as it opened and closed again. It was a truly impressive sight.

The 20th century was to add not one but two new aqueducts, both in the same place. In the 1930s the increase in London traffic gave rise to a demand for a relief road to take through traffic away from the centre. The result was the North Circular Road – the South Circular was always something of a travesty, simply a linking together of old routes. But the North Circular was a new construction and the Grand Union Canal was in the way, so it had to be carried across the new road on a concrete aqueduct. Few Londoners were even aware it existed, as it appeared to be just another concrete bridge across the busy commuter route, though it was always more noticeable in winter, when it was frequently festooned with icicles. 60 years on and the North Circular had become something of a

LEFT: The original Barton aqueduct was demolished to make way for the Manchester Ship Canal and replaced by the present swing aqueduct.

nightmare for motorists, particularly commuters, so more road improvements were called for, and that meant the old aqueduct needed replacing. This involved a brand-new technology. It was

LEFT: The Barton aqueduct swung to the side to allow a vessel to pass on the Ship Canal.

prefabricated and as the old was demolished, the new was slid into place. An unusual feature is that the waterway has a central island, with channels to either side. It is perhaps not the loveliest aqueduct on the system, but its construction would certainly have impressed and even amazed the earlier generations of canal engineers.

PLACES TO VISIT

The following are among the most imposing aqueducts in Britain.

ALMOND: The aqueduct carrying the Union Canal over the river is located just south of the B7030 at Ratho, 10 miles west of Edinburgh. Aqueduct car park EH28 8LQ.

BARTON: This swing aqueduct crosses the Manchester Ship Canal at Chapel Place, Urmston, Manchester, Greater Manchester M41 7LE. The abutments of the original stone aqueduct are also visible.

DUNDAS: The aqueduct crosses the River Avon near Brassknocker Hill, Monkton Combe, Bath BA2 7JD. It can also be reached via a passenger boat from Bath.

ENGINE ARM: An aqueduct on the Wolverhampton level of the Birmingham Canal, at Rolfe Street, Warley B68 2AF.

HAZELHURST: The aqueduct carries the Leek branch of the Caldon Canal over the main line close to the Hollybush Inn, Denford ST13 7JT.

LONGDON: Situated just off the B5063, Longdon-upon-Tern TF6 6LJ.

LUNE: The aqueduct carries the Lancaster Canal across the river at Lancaster, passing to the east of the city centre. Car park at Caton Road LA1 3PE.

MARPLE: The aqueduct crosses the River Goyt at the bottom of the Marple flight of locks, Lockside Road, Marple SK6 6BN.

PONTCYSYLLTE: There are three possible ways to view this aqueduct. The first is to take the A5 east from Llangollen to Froncysyllte, which gives you a view down on to it: a particularly good vantage point is from the Aqueduct Inn, Holyhead Road LL20 7PY. The alternative is to take the B5103 from Llangollen and then take the minor road to the right that brings you right under the aqueduct. The third option is to take the horse-drawn trip boat from Llangollen wharf, which takes you across the aqueduct.

CHAPTER 5

TUNNELS, CUTTINGS AND BANKS

For many people, canal tunnels are little more than dark, dank holes through a hill. There is a lot more to them than that – and to canal engineers responsible for their construction, they could be a nightmare. It started right at the beginning of the canal age, when Brindley, faced with the prospect of digging through Harecastle Hill on the Trent and Mersey Canal, felt compelled to halve the ideal width. One problem was that he had no model to follow. It was true that miners were accustomed to tunnelling deep underground, and indeed the Bridgewater Canal boats could penetrate deep into the mines of Worsley Delph through a labyrinth of tunnels. But mine tunnels and canal tunnels have a fundamental difference. The miners followed the coal seam and it made no difference whether it took them north, south, east or west. The canal tunnel had to be dug in just one specific direction and ideally should run in a completely straight line from end to end.

Tunnel construction

The direction was predetermined by the line of the canal as a whole and could be marked out on the surface of the hill, but transferring that line to the underground workings was far more difficult. For a long tunnel, a number of shafts would be sunk, so that work could carry on from the openings at either end and also outwards from the foot of

LEFT: The southern end of Harecastle Tunnel and the fan house surrounding the entrance that supplies ventilation for those making the long journey through.

each shaft. So, the first essential was to ensure that all the shafts were at the correct depth, which meant getting an accurate profile of the hill. The surveyors' main tools were the chain and the theodolite. The chain, as its name suggests, is a series of links that extend for exactly 22 yards (20m) – a length actually known as a chain. Armed with a set of graduated poles, the surveyor set each pole a chain away from the last, then lined up the marks with the theodolite. This gave the angle of the slope, and knowing the distance apart of the poles, a simple calculation gave the vertical rise in the surface. So if, for example, a site had been chosen for a shaft, then the survey gave the height above the base line at canal level and that

determined how deep the shaft had to be dug to line up precisely with the entrance. The methods were crude but on the whole they worked.

The other problem facing the engineer was that he had only the vaguest idea of the conditions he would meet as the workers drove ever deeper into the hillside. The main obstacle was water that flooded into the workings. At Harecastle, it was at first kept at bay by means of wind- and water-powered pumps. When these proved unable to cope, a steam engine had to be brought in. This was of a type based on the earliest form of steam pump developed at the beginning of the 18th century by Thomas Newcomen. It depended on admitting steam into a cylinder below a piston,

then condensing the steam by spraying with cold water, at which point atmospheric pressure would force the piston down. The piston was fastened to one end of an overhead beam and pump rods were attached to the other. As the piston was pushed down the rods were raised and then, pressure equalised, the weight of the rods dragged them down again. The huge engine nodded day and night above the tunnel.

Work on the tunnel was far from easy – the water turned the ground into quicksand, while elsewhere there was hard rock to be removed by blasting with gunpowder. Work that began in high optimism in 1766 was only completed in 1777, by which time Brindley was dead. The original tunnel is no longer

ABOVE: The northern end of the second Harecastle Tunnel on the Trent and Mersey Canal, engineered by Thomas Telford. The original Brindley tunnel is no longer in use.

in use. As traffic increased, the narrow tunnel, which had no room for boats to pass each other, had become a bottleneck. Telford was commissioned to build a second tunnel alongside the first, the idea being that the old tunnel would carry traffic in one direction and the new in the opposite. Seeing the entrances of the two side by side, the contrast is remarkable. The original, low and narrow, is uninviting, promising a claustrophobic journey.

The new is broad, high and has the luxury of a towpath, mounted on brackets on a side wall. At least Telford, who was in charge of building the second tunnel, could appreciate the difficulties faced by Brindley. In a report, he described the various types of ground through which the tunnel had to be forced:

'The ground is of different and various kinds: such as Rock, Sand, Coal Measures and other kinds of Earth – very tedious to encounter with. The Rock I find to be extremely hard, some of it in my opinion is much harder than ever any Tunnel has been driven in before – excepting the one that is executed by the side of it.'

When later engineers criticised the workmanship of the original tunnel, they should perhaps have been more aware of the difficulties faced by Brindley. John Rennie had inspected the old tunnel and described it as 'small and crooked with bad brickwork'. There are no records of where the bricks for the tunnel lining came from, but they could well have been made on site, which was not unusual for such major projects. The bricks were fired in clamps instead of kilns. The raw bricks are built up in an arch, with a space for the fire at the bottom and spaces left between the bricks for the heat to permeate the whole structure. In effect, the bricks themselves form the actual kiln.

Although we cannot go through the original Harecastle tunnel, there are three more narrow tunnels on the canal that are still in use. Boating through them, it is very obvious that the alignments are far from perfect, with distinct kinks along the way. But when Brindley came to build them there were no real precedents to draw on and the difficulties the engineer faced were formidable – and he would have had little idea what to expect. The science of geology simply did not exist at that time: in fact, it could be said to have its origins in canal tunnelling. William Smith was an engineer on the Somerset Coal Canal in 1799 and he noticed the different strata of rock that appeared as work went on and deduced they might represent different time periods. He became known as 'Strata' Smith and 'the Father of English Geology'.

Variety in tunnel design

There is perhaps more variety in tunnels than one might expect. Although it has long been disused thanks to a collapse, one of the most imposing is to be found at Sapperton on the Thames and Severn Canal. It is the grandest tunnel in Britain, but not the longest – that honour goes to Standedge on the Huddersfield Narrow Canal. At 3,817 yards (2.17 miles/3,490m) long, Sapperton takes second place, but where the Yorkshire tunnel was built for narrow boats, Sapperton was built to take barges, so is 15 feet wide and 15 feet high at the crown (4.6m x 4.6m). It is horseshoe-shaped in cross section, with a floor of puddled clay. Unlike Harecastle, the tunnel was said to be so straight that you could see right through from end to end. It was an immense work – in all, 25 shafts were sunk and it required a large workforce. Unusually, the company provided good accommodation for the workers with a three-storey house at the Coates end, which was converted into a hotel when the tunnel was completed in 1789. Since then it has lost the top storey in a fire, but it is still a pub today, The Tunnel House. Close to the pub is the very grand portico at the tunnel entrance, built in the neoclassical style, with pillars, roundels and round-headed niches. At the opposite end, at Sapperton, the portal is less dramatic, with simple castellations. There was a company building at this end as well, which became the Bricklayers Arms, now The Daneway.

It is possible to travel a short distance into the tunnel at the Coates end, and it provides a fascinating insight into the nature of the tunnel and the ground through which it passes. Once inside, one can see the puddled clay floor through the clear water, and the first section is lined. Then a far more interesting section appears where the tunnel has been blasted through the

RIGHT: The classical entrance to Sapperton Tunnel at Daneway.

rock. Here, the 'roof' is formed of great slabs of limestone, the actual bedrock. In the sides, semicircular grooves are visible. These were made during construction. In order to blast a way through the rock, the workers had to drill holes by hand, pack them with gunpowder, tamp it firmly into place with a metal rod, apply a fuse, light it and get out at high speed. The grooves are the remaining halves of the drill holes. We have no full accounts of what it was like to work in a tunnel such as this, but there is a contemporary illustration showing navvies in the Regent's Canal tunnel at Islington. In the distance is centring on which the arch of the lining is being laid. The workers, stripped to the waist, only have flares for lighting. One man is pushing a small wagon of spoil along a simple rail track on the tunnel floor, and the body of the truck can be detached and hauled up a shaft. The scene at Sapperton could well have been similar.

LEFT: A rare illustration showing the Islington Tunnel under construction. Spoil is being moved on rails and up the shaft, the whole scene lit by flares. In the background, men are constructing the arched lining.

BELOW: Islington Tunnel on the Regent's Canal. Apart from the graffiti, it is hard to believe this is in the heart of London.

If Sapperton is the grandest tunnel, then Dudley is certainly the most interesting to visit. It has its origins in the short Lord Ward's Canal, named after its promoter, Viscount Dudley and Ward. He owned extensive mines under Castle Hill, producing coal, limestone and fireclay, all essential raw materials or the iron industry. The arrival of the Birmingham Canal close to the mines made it sound economic sense to promote a canal to join them to the new water highway. Built in 1775, a large part of the canal consisted of a 226-yard (207m) tunnel, linking directly with the mines. That was just the start for what was to become a labyrinth of tunnels serving the mines and quarries deep underground, which would eventually stretch for some 3 miles (5km).

The scene then shifted to the opposite end of the hill, when work began on linking the system to the newly constructed Stourbridge Canal via a new tunnel. Eventually, this would become a through route, known simply as the Dudley Canal Tunnel. But there is nothing simple about this underground system, as a journey on one of the special trip boats from the Black Country Living Museum soon makes clear. Because the tunnel was built long before the age of engines and motors, there was no allowance made for ventilation, so electric boats are used, and electric tugs are provided for anyone taking their own boat through. This journey starts as the trip boats do, at the Birmingham end of the tunnel.

The first section to be reached is the original Lord Ward Tunnel, which is brick-lined and unusual in having quite a shallow arched entrance. In the

TOP: The southern end of Dudley Tunnel: the device hung in the entrance warns boaters that the tunnel inside is both lower and narrower and indicates the maximum size of boat that can get through.

BOTTOM: A trip boat taking visitors towards the low narrow entrance at the northern end of Dudley Tunnel.

lined section of the tunnel there is evidence of how it was constructed in the gaps in the brickwork, which originally held scaffolding. These were often left as 'weep holes', allowing water to escape from behind the brickwork. They also provide a clue to the local geology, as many of the holes have calciferous deposits, like frozen drapery, sticking to the wall beneath them. The first section opens out into Shirt Mill Basin, with wharves for loading the boats with material brought to the basin via side tunnels leading to the stone and coal mines. After this brief visit to the open air, a second short length of lined tunnel leads out under a great rock arch to reach Castle Mill Basin. This marks the end of the original construction period, and was once a roofed cave, but has long since been opened out to the sky. Three tunnels meet here, including the branch to more extensive limestone workings at Wren's Nest Hill, which then leads on to the main tunnel complex.

The main tunnel at the far side of the basin is the section on which work began in January 1786. At first it runs through bare rock, passing through an area where the strata of Wenlock Shale can be seen running at an angle of 45 degrees to the horizontal. Then the whole tunnel opens out into its most spectacular feature, the Cathedral Arch. The name is apt, for this waterway junction is covered by a great vault rising 30 feet (9m) above the water. Once again, this is a point where a now abandoned system of canals led to yet more mines and quarries. For the rest of the way, the narrow, low tunnel alternates between lined sections and exposed rock surfaces – shales, limestone and two varieties of sandstone are all visible. As at Sapperton, one can see signs of holes drilled for blasting. Construction shafts still punctuate the journey, and although they have all now been capped they still drip relentlessly on to the passing boats, and their sides are covered in mineral deposits. The brick lining is a patchwork of old, rough red bricks and more modern blue engineering bricks. In places, the roof lowers right down, and the boat seems to squeeze through like a finger in a glove. The end arrives at the southern portal at Parkhead, reconstructed almost a century

TOP: Leggers working a narrow boat through a tunnel. This was the only way of moving through tunnels without towpaths, before motor boats were introduced.

BOTTOM: An 18th-century illustration showing a boatman poling his boat across Castle Basin, part of the Dudley Tunnel complex.

after work first began, having been rebuilt in 1884 using Staffordshire blue bricks. Working boats through the tunnel must always have been difficult, with no towpath. In the narrow sections, boats would have been 'legged' through, the boatmen lying on their backs, their feet against the tunnel walls and then walking their way along. In the open sections, they would have had to use poles to push the boats across.

Standedge Tunnel on the Huddersfield Narrow Canal was also built without a towpath, which meant that boats had to be legged through the whole of its 5,702 yards (3.24 miles/5.2km). It was an immense project, begun in 1794 and not completed until 1811. This was only partly due to engineering difficulties: most of the long delays came when the company ran out of money. Like other canal tunnels, this was worked from a number of shafts and three powerful steam engines were brought into use. It does have some interesting features. When the railway arrived, the line from Huddersfield to Manchester also needed to tunnel under Standedge Fell, and the new tunnel was built right alongside the canal tunnel. Short connecting tunnels were built so that spoil from the railway tunnel could be moved to the canal. This was all good news for the railway but not for boatmen on the canal. Historian Charles Hadfield told me of a trip he made through the tunnel, in the days of steam locomotives: every time an engine passed on the railway, he was choked by the smoke. Today, there is a trip boat working the tunnel and a small museum at the Marsden end. It is also possible to get an idea of the scale of the operation by following the path of the tunnel over the bleak moorland of Standedge Fell, where one can still find remains of engine houses and heaps of spoil.

The southern end of Netherton Tunnel. The engine house at the top of the hill once housed a steam engine that pumped water from a local colliery.

Challenges of tunnel building

There are tunnels throughout the system, long and short, shallow and deep underground, and each has its own story to tell. In the early years, tunnelling was the only way to cope with rising ground that couldn't be got round. On the Oxford Canal, Brindley was forced to drive a 1,138-yard (1km) long tunnel at Fenny Compton. It was inevitably narrow with no towpath, but there were sections that broadened out to allow boats to pass, and iron rings were set into the walls to allow boats to be hauled along. It was, however, a major inconvenience, and in 1838 the company bought the land above the tunnel and opened it up to create a deep cutting with just a short section still in a tunnel, and even this was later removed. The present cutting is still referred to as Fenny Compton Tunnel. A later generation of engineers would probably never have even considered tunnelling and dug the cutting from the start.

William Jessop, the chief engineer on the Grand Junction Canal, was faced with the task of finding a way through the Chiltern Hills that lay right across the path of the canal. His solution was to dig a cutting at Tring that would run for a mile and a half (2.4km) and at its deepest would be 30 feet (9m) below the natural level of the ground. This immense undertaking all had to be done by hand,

RIGHT: The eastern end of Standedge Tunnel at Marsden. Britain's longest canal tunnel, it had no towpath so in the early days boats had to be legged through.

BELOW: The interior of Newbold Tunnel on the Oxford Canal.

by a huge workforce armed only with pickaxe, spade and barrow, with black powder for blasting where necessary. One thing that made life easier was that these are chalk hills, not made of harder rock. Even so, the work was arduous and hundreds of men were employed.

There is a special problem associated with deep cuttings: how to dispose of the spoil. The answer was barrow runs. All along the side of the cutting planks were laid over trestles, reaching from top to bottom. Horses at the top of the cutting were harnessed by ropes passing over pulleys to the barrowload of spoil at the bottom. Once the barrow was full, the signal was given for the horse to move away from the rim. The navvy would balance the barrow in front of him as he made his way up the

greasy plank. Accidents were inevitable. If a man lost his footing or the barrow slipped, all he could do was try to fling the barrow to one side of the plank and himself to the other. We have a good idea of how the scene could have looked because when Robert Stephenson came to build the London and Birmingham Railway he too needed a cutting at Tring, and we have pictures of the barrow runs in use in the railway cutting. Once work at Tring was finished, this would have been a startling white chalky gash in the landscape, but over the years the cutting has been covered by rich vegetation of bushes and shrubs, making it an attractive green corridor.

The scale of work at Tring is impressive, but the cutting at Laggan on the Caledonian Canal was on an even vaster scale. Here, we are fortunate in having a first-hand account of the work by the poet Robert Southey, who was taken by Telford on a tour of the construction sites. A rather more sophisticated system was in use than the barrow runs of Tring:

LEFT: The Oxford Canal at Fenny Compton was originally in a tunnel, but it was later opened out to create this cutting.

BELOW: The Grand Union Canal carving through the Chilterns at Tring cutting.

'The earth is removed by horses walking along the bench of the Canal, and drawing the laden cartlets up one inclined plane, while the empty ones which are connected with them by a chain passing over pulleys, are let down another. This was going on in numberless places and such a mess of earth had been thrown up on both sides along the whole line, that the men appeared in the proportion of emmets to an ant-hill, amid their own work. The hour of rest for men and horses is announced by blowing a horn; and so well have the horses learned to measure time by their own exertions and sense of fatigue, that if the signal be delayed five minutes they stop of their own accord, without it.'

Paradoxically, although the scale of the ship canal is so much greater than the Grand Junction, the cutting seems less impressive. The sides do not seem to close you in when travelling through by boat in the way that those at Tring do. But walking above the cutting the true scale is far more apparent, not least because of the huge quantities of spoil piled up along the rim. And down on the water the modern pleasure boats that mostly use the canal look like toys. However, visually the most dramatic cuttings are to be found on what is now the main line of the Shropshire Union.

The canal was built in the face of a growing threat from a new, rival form of transport – the steam railway. The Canal Act was passed in 1826, just one year after the opening of the Stockton and Darlington Railway. As it was intended to form a new efficient link between Liverpool and Birmingham, it was essential that it should take as direct a route as possible, and if that involved massive earthworks, then so be it. But the problems encountered in the

BELOW: The Clyde Puffer VIC 32 steaming through the deep Laggan cutting on the Caledonian Canal.

works were far greater than anyone anticipated. At Cowley, for example. it was originally intended to cut a 600-yard (549m) tunnel through the rock. But the rock proved to be such wretched stuff that the tunnel was reduced to a mere 81 yards (74m), with the rest as a deep rock cutting. However, the major problems came with the two most imposing cuttings – Woodseaves and Grub Street. These were dug with steep sides and to great depths, but they proved incredibly difficult to stabilise. Time and time again, the earth and rock would slide back. Success was achieved at last, and now the earth that was once so treacherous is covered by vegetation. In summer, travelling through these cuttings is like passing through a green tunnel and the foliage is so luxuriant one could be in an Amazonian rainforest. The high bridges that cross the cutting only seem to increase the sense of isolation, of being in a little world of one's own. The rest of the world is up there, but out of sight.

A troublesome endeavour

The Shropshire Union is not only notable for its deep cuttings but also for its high banks, a normal part of the technique of cut and fill, in which spoil from the cut is used to build the bank. They are not such obviously major engineering works as the cuttings, but when seen from the surrounding countryside, their massive scale is more impressive. The Shelmore embankment is pierced by a tunnel to carry a local road, and that helps to give a sense of scale. The construction of cut and fill gave even more headaches to the engineers than the cuttings

BELOW: Cowley cutting on the Shropshire Union was originally intended to be a tunnel, but the ground was unsuitable.

and it was Shelmore Bank that proved most troublesome of all. What would have made it even more infuriating for Telford was the fact that there was no engineering necessity for it to be built at all. The obvious line lay through Shelmore Wood, part of the estate owned by Lord Anson, and it was here that his lordship's pheasants were reared. He was sufficiently powerful to insist that the canal went round rather than through his property. And that involved the construction of the great – and greatly troublesome – bank.

Work began at the beginning of 1831 and soon there were between 300 and 400 hundred men on site and as many as 70 horses bringing the spoil to the great curving embankment. The trouble was that the earth kept slipping. Telford realised that the rich marl that was being used was actually collapsing under its own weight. It was squeezing out the sides of the bank. He decided to bring in a different sort of sandy soil from elsewhere in the workings. It was only the first of several solutions to the slippage problem, none of which resulted in the hoped-for stabilisation. By January 1833,

BELOW: Burnley embankment carries the Leeds and Liverpool Canal for nearly a mile above the old mill town.

Telford was showing signs of being worn out by his years of unremitting hard work, and for the first time was unable to compile his annual report. A new man was brought in as chief engineer, William Cubitt. The new engineer had little more success than Telford, and the opening of the whole canal had to be delayed more than once. The work was finally completed in March 1835. Telford was not there to see it: he had died the previous year. Embankments might not seem the most exciting works on the canal, but they represent immense efforts, as the Shelmore story vividly illustrates.

The one thing that banks do afford us today is a bird's eye view of the countryside. It may be of a rural landscape, as on the Shropshire Union, or it could provide a panorama of the industrial past, as the great bank at Burnley on the Leeds and Liverpool Canal does as it rides high above the old cotton mills of the town. But one thing is true of all the great earthworks – tunnels, cuttings and embankments: they are a tribute to what can be achieved without the benefit of modern technology.

We have not quite finished with looking at the various essential elements that went into the making of canals. One vital ingredient is still missing – water to feed them.

TUNNELS IN ORDER OF LENGTH

STANDEDGE: Huddersfield Narrow Canal, 5,702 yards (3.24 miles/5.2km). It runs from Marsden to Diggle, with a visitor centre and boat trips at Waters Road, Marsden HD7 6NQ.

SAPPERTON: Thames and Severn Canal, 3,817 yards (2.17 miles/3.5km). It runs from Sapperton, approached from the Daneway pub GL7 6LN to Coates.

DUDLEY: Dudley No 1, 3,177 yards (1.79 miles/2.9km). It begins at what is now the Black Country Living Museum, Tipton Road, Dudley DY1 4SQ, from where boat trips through the tunnel are run. It ends at Parkhead.

BLISWORTH: Grand Union Canal, 3,046 yards (1.74 miles/2.8km). The tunnel is named after the village of Blisworth at the northern end but is better approached from Stoke Bruerne, a small canal settlement that includes a canal museum – Stoke Bruerne, Towcester NN12 7SE.

NETHERTON: BCN Netherton Branch, 3,027 yards (1.72 miles/2.8km) The tunnel was built to parallel the Dudley Canal to avoid congestion, and was wide enough for narrow boats to pass. The northern portal is close to Dudley Port on the Birmingham main line. The southern portal is at Windmill End DY2 9HS.

PLACES TO VISIT

DUDLEY TUNNEL BOAT TRIPS, Dudley Canal, Birmingham New Road, Dudley DY1 4SB.

SAPPERTON TUNNEL, Thames and Severn Canal, Coates, Nr. Cirencester GL7 6PW.

STANDEDGE TUNNEL VISITOR CENTRE, Waters Road, Marsden HD7 6NQ.

GRUB STREET CUTTING, Shropshire Union Canal, High Offley, Stafford ST20 0NG.

LAGGAN CUTTING, Caledonian Canal, Laggan PH34 4EB.

CHAPTER 6

WATER SUPPLY

Life would be simple for canal engineers if, once the work was complete, all they had to do was fill the channel up and that would be it for the foreseeable future. Unfortunately, reality is very different. Consider what is known as a summit canal – one that starts at perhaps a river, climbs up to the highest level, then after a while drops down again to the far end. As a boat makes its way up the locks, it will need to fill each lock with water from the upper level, and so on until it reaches the summit. Now there is no water higher up, apart from the summit pound. On leaving the summit, it will drain off another lock full. Unless the water in the top pound is replaced it will run dry, and that means supplying a lot of water. Even on a narrow canal, each boat passing over the summit will be using over 50,000 gallons (189,270 litres). The problem is less severe when there is a very long summit pound that can act as a reservoir, as for example with the long pound that begins at the top of the Bingley Five on the Leeds and Liverpool, but few canals enjoy that luxury.

Pumping stations

One solution is to take the water from existing sources, such as streams, rivers, lakes and ponds. This is fine in theory but not always practical in practice, and nowhere is this better illustrated than on the Kennet and Avon. At the Bath end, the canal climbs steeply from the River Avon, until it reaches a level above the river, where it remains lock-free right through to Bradford on Avon. This is a barge canal with broad locks, so the water loss is roughly twice that of the narrow canals, as water from the summit eventually gets lost in the Avon. The obvious source of replacement is the river itself, but by the time the top pound is reached, the canal is high above the river. The answer provided by the canal's engineer, John Rennie, was Claverton pumping station.

There was an old water mill down by the river, with the typical arrangement of a weir, with water diverted down a leat to turn the wheels. At Rennie's suggestion, the company bought the

LEFT: There was no problem with water supply on the Bridgewater Canal, which was fed by drainage water from the Worsley mines. The water was stained by minerals, hence the tomato-soup appearance of the canal at Worsley Delph.

mill and instead of using the waterwheels to drive machinery for grinding corn, they adapted them for working pumps. At one side of the main building is a pair of breast-shot waterwheels, magnificent devices, each 15 feet (4.6m) in diameter and 11 feet (3.4m) wide, turning on the same axle. They work through gearing to operate the beam pump. The power of the river itself is used to lift the water up the hillside and into the canal. It began operating in 1813 and thanks to the efforts of volunteers who restored it, everything is now back in full working order and the site is regularly opened to the public. And if necessary – when, for example, there is a power failure and the electric pump now used is unavailable – the old pump can still be used just as it was two centuries ago.

BELOW: The Ellesmere Canal was supplied by water from above Horseshoe Falls on the River Dee. It was passed into the navigable feeder canal that runs through Llangollen to join the main line at Pontcysyllte.

At the Kennet end of the canal, the situation was more complicated as there was no obvious natural source of water. But a number of springs were available and these were used to create the pond of Wilton Water. There remained the problem of raising the water to canal level and the answer this time was the Crofton Pumping Station. An adit was dug from Wilton Water to create a well beneath the station. The actual work of lifting that water and feeding it into the canal was done by a pair of steam beam engines. At first a second-hand engine was installed, but later two new engines replaced it. The older of the two was built by the famous manufacturer Boulton and Watt and installed in 1812, the year Napoleon's defeated army was struggling to abandon their Russian campaign. It is the oldest steam engine still to be seen in its original site and able to do the job it was installed to do in the first place. It is worth looking at this engine in more detail because engines such as this were crucial to the Industrial Revolution and the development of canals.

The early Newcomen engine was briefly described in the previous chapter. It did the job of pumping but was extremely inefficient in terms of fuel. This did not matter when it was being used to drain coal mines, but at other places it was extremely expensive to run. It was James Watt who identified the fundamental problem. When the cylinder was sprayed to condense the steam, a lot of energy had to be applied to heat the cylinder up again. The answer might seem mundane and obvious, but it was of immense importance. He cooled down the steam in a separate condenser, so that the cylinder could be kept permanently hot. There was, however, a snag. In the Newcomen engine, it was air pressing down on the piston in the open-topped cylinder that made it move – but heat was being lost through the opening. The next step was crucial. He closed the cylinder top and used the expansive power of steam under pressure to do

BELOW: An old water mill beside the River Avon was converted into a water-powered pumping station to lift water from the river up to the Kennet and Avon Canal.

the work. The atmospheric engine had become a genuine steam engine.

In 1848 a second engine was added, this time built by the Cornish company Harvey of Hayle. The No. 2 engine was rebuilt in 1903 and visiting the site today nothing much has changed since then. The story starts at the back of the building in the boiler house. Originally, the Boulton and Watt engine would have been supplied with steam using a waggon boiler, so called because it was roughly the shape of a covered waggon. This has long since been replaced by the more efficient Lancashire boiler, but one thing hasn't changed – it still needs to be fired by hand and shooting a shovelful of coal into the open firebox door requires skill as well as muscle power. From here, steam passes to the cylinder of one of the engines with its array of gleaming metal handles. These are used to control the opening and closing of the valves when starting up the engine – once under way, it becomes automatic. The piston is connected to one end of

the overhead beam, which can be seen from the beam gallery. The Boulton and Watt beam weighs a massive 8 tons yet seems to move effortlessly in its slow see-sawing action. The opposite end of the beam is connected to the pump rod. At the bottom of the building is the condenser, into which the exhaust steam from the cylinder is passed. Each of the engines lifts the water to a height of 40 feet (12m) above the well and sends it out in gushes to the feeder that carries it away to the canal, at the impressive rate of 245 gallons (1,114 litres) for each stroke, so with both at work 490 gallons (2,228 litres) is delivered for each nod of the great beams.

Up in the beam gallery is a device that is fascinating to watch; it is of immense historic importance and goes by the prosaic name of Watt's parallel motion. In the old Newcomen engine, the beam was attached to the piston by a chain that pulled the end of the beam down. But chains can only pull, not push – so a different

ABOVE: The second pumping station for the Kennet and Avon, at Crofton, used a pair of steam engines to pump water up to the summit level.

RIGHT: Steam at Crofton is raised by means of the coal-fired Lancashire boiler.

force was needed to pull down the opposite end. This was supplied by the pump rods. Because the Watt engine used steam power, the steam could be admitted either below or above the piston, moving it in either direction. So, it was possible to push or pull, but there was a problem with the beam engine: the end of the beam moved along the arc of a circle, while the piston moved vertically. Watt solved the difficulty by attaching the connecting rod to one corner of a shifting parallelogram of metal rods. Now the engine was double acting, and the opposite end of the beam no longer needed a separate force to move it. So, instead of pump rods, it might be attached to a long arm and a crank and then used to turn a wheel. And if you can turn a wheel, then you can use it to power machinery, just as the waterwheel was doing in 18th-century textile mills.

This innovation had a profound effect on canal development. The new steam mills needed to be fed with vast quantities of coal – and the most efficient way of delivering it from the collieries was by water. This encouraged development in the burgeoning industrial areas, and increased traffic meant an even greater need for adequate water supplies.

Steam engines were already in use before Crofton was built. The old main line of the Birmingham Canal was supplied by water using two Boulton and Watt engines, one of which was situated close to the company's factory at Smethwick. Built in 1779, it was later replaced and the new pump house is now home to the Galton Valley Canal Museum in the deep Smethwick cutting. The original engine has been preserved, restored and put back into working order. It is regularly steamed at Thinktank, the Birmingham Science Museum.

There were many engines and engine houses around the system, but one deserves special mention – Leawood pumping station on the Cromford Canal. It stands at the end of the aqueduct over the River Derwent and was used to pump water up from the river into the canal. Originally, the canal was supplied by water from the Cromford Sough, which drained a local lead mine and also provided water for Sir Richard Arkwright's cotton mill at Cromford. But then Arkwright lost the rights to use the water in a court case, and the canal also suffered. A new steam pump was ordered in 1845 but was not ready for use until 1850.

The engine house is a handsome building, built of rusticated stone, with dressed stone at the quoins and surrounding the round-headed windows. The door is flanked by pilasters and topped by a pediment. There is a tall chimney with an unusually wide parapet at the top. The engine inside, which has been restored, is massive, with a 59-inch (1.5m) diameter cylinder that stands 10 feet (3m) high. It was able to deliver 899 gallons (4,087 litres) at a stroke. The site is regularly opened for visitors.

Reservoirs

In some cases, natural sources such as springs and streams could be used as feeders. In the Pennines, there is seldom a water shortage and streams from the hills could be allowed to run down into the canal, though it was always necessary for the water to run first into a small basin to hold back sediment. The original idea for supplying water for the summit level of the Grand Junction was to make use of numerous springs in the Wendover area. They would be diverted into a feeder and it was decided that it made sense to make the feeder navigable, and so it became the Wendover Arm, terminating in a wharf at the town. It did not turn out well. There was considerable leakage from the branch canal, water seeping away through the chalk. A more reliable source was needed and it was decided to construct three reservoirs – Marsworth, Tringford and Startops. Two of the three were actually below the level of the canal so water had to be lifted by steam pumps. A fourth reservoir was added later, but it is Marsworth, at the end of Tring cutting and close to the canal, that is most obvious to anyone boating in the area. It is now a Site of Special Scientific Interest, particularly known for its birdlife and also popular with local fishermen.

Among the most extensive users of reservoirs was the Rochdale Canal, which took a direct route over the Pennine hills, involving the construction of 92 locks, each able to take barges or a pair of narrow boats. There was only a short summit level in a cutting, so water supply was always going to be a problem. The canal passed through a region where the local textile mills depended on water power, so no source could be used that would affect them. The only answer was reservoirs. Originally, there were two, at Hollingworth and Blackstone Edge, but a third was later added in the Chelburn valley. The engineer, William Jessop, also took careful measures to make water use as efficient

RIGHT: Leawood steam-powered pumping station stands at the end of the Derwent aqueduct on the Cromford Canal.

as possible by ensuring that the rise and fall was roughly the same for each lock, so that the same quantity of water was constantly being passed into each pound.

These were massive undertakings. The dam for the Hollingworth reservoir was built 14 feet (4.3m) wide at the top to take a roadway and was constructed with a 1:2 slope. At its heart was a 9-foot-thick (2.7m) core of puddled clay. It was utilitarian but was certainly no eyesore. In fact, by the middle of the 18th century it had been renamed Hollingworth Lake and had become a popular holiday resort, with hotels for guests built on the banks. Many reservoirs proved popular attractions in later years. Between 1797 and 1798, one was constructed to feed the Caldon Canal. It attracted visitors and one couple were so charmed by the spot that they named their son after it. It was Rudyard Lake and the family were the Kiplings.

Sometimes the fact that these were canal reservoirs is forgotten. When Telford devised the new straight main line Birmingham Canal, a large reservoir had to be constructed, originally called Rotton Park but now known as Edgbaston Reservoir. Some years ago, there were letters of complaint because the canal was taking water out of the anglers' lake. It had to be pointed out that without the canal their fishing lake would never have existed. It is an indication of the value so many canal reservoirs have had for local communities; however, it always has to be remembered that they were not built for pleasure, but to ensure that the vital trade of the waterways could continue uninterrupted by drought.

PUMPING STATIONS OPEN TO THE PUBLIC

CLAVERTON: Ferry Lane, Claverton, Bath BA2 7BH. www.claverton.org.uk

CROFTON: Crofton, Marlborough SN8 3DW. www.croftonbeamengines.org

LEAWOOD: High Peak Junction Visitor Centre, Lea Bridge, Cromford DE4 5HN. The pumping station is a quarter of a mile walk away. www.middleton-leawood.org.uk

GALTON VALLEY CANAL MUSEUM: Canalside off Brasshouse Lane, Smethwick B66 18A. www.sandwell.gov.uk/info/200265/museums_and_art_gallery/10/our_museums

HOLLINGWORTH LAKE, reservoir for Rochdale Canal: Rakewood Road, Littleborough OL15 0AQ.

FAR LEFT: Mechanism for controlling a sluice at Marsworth reservoir.

LEFT: Marsworth reservoir was built to supply water to the Grand Junction Canal at the northern end of Tring cutting.

OVERLEAF: The Grand Junction reservoirs supplied water to the canal through the feeder, which was made navigable and is now the Wendover Arm of the Grand Union Canal.

THE WENDOVER ARM

GRAND UNION CANAL

1793   1993

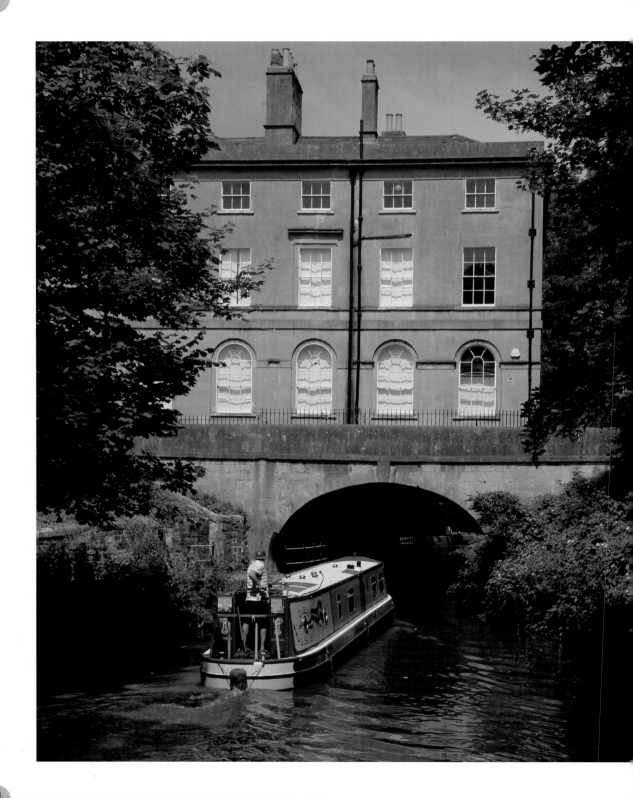

CHAPTER 7

COMPANY PROPERTIES AND STRUCTURES

Once a canal was completed and open for trade, the canal company's priorities changed. Now their efforts had to be concentrated on ensuring it remained open and that they could go about the serious business of collecting revenue from its users to repay the construction costs and, with luck, begin making a profit for the shareholders. This required administrators and administrators need offices.

Canal offices

The Kennet and Avon Canal offices were originally housed in a splendid Georgian house in Bath, situated on the road that crosses the short Cleveland tunnel, just to the east of Sydney Gardens. Today, it scarcely attracts any special attention from those walking the city streets – just one more beautiful building among so many.

But Georgian elegance was not limited to the city that is famous for it. As mentioned earlier, Thomas Telford had always been interested in architecture and at Ellesmere he designed the company headquarters, Beech House, in a style that is a grander version of the Grindley Brook lock

LEFT: The former offices of the Kennet and Avon Company were housed in this typical Georgian building, straddling the canal in Bath.

cottage, with a prominent bay at the front. This extends for two storeys, giving the effect of a turret at the front of the house. It is a handsome building in an attractive setting and, like the Bath offices, very much of its time. Not all office buildings carry things off quite so stylishly. The offices of the Stroudwater Canal in Stroud look fine when seen from the front, with a smooth stucco finish, but this is just that – a front, behind which lurks a rather plain brick building. It is always a tricky balancing act, between decorative elegance and pomposity. The company office at the Leeds end of the Leeds and Liverpool Canal, for example, carries it off with style. Although it is quite a small building, it is given the full neoclassical treatment. It works because the anonymous architect had a good eye for proportion. At the other end of the scale, you have to travel north to Scotland to Port Dundas on the Forth and Clyde Canal. The company offices have all the appearance of a country mansion. A central bay, topped by a pediment, contains the entrance

One of the more unusual company buildings was the Tontine Hotel at Stourport, built to house visiting merchants.

with a porch carried on classical pillars. Windows are tall and gracious and the whole is beautifully proportioned.

A number of other office buildings have survived, but some have become isolated from the canals they once served. The Oxford Canal once terminated in a large basin near the centre of Oxford, and it was here that the company had their offices. But as trade on the canal declined, the basin was filled in and Nuffield College built on the site. The old offices are tucked away down a lane but well worth seeking out, if only for the carved company coat of arms over the portico. It features Britannia holding a shield bearing the Oxford coat of arms, while behind her the canal sweeps past the rotunda of the University library, the Radcliffe Camera. The fact that the canal never actually went near that grand building obviously didn't bother the designer of the arms.

Some of the grandest offices were lost when the canals were nationalised and old companies ceased to exist. But not all went into public ownership. Most of the Rochdale Canal had been abandoned, but a short section through Manchester remained in use as a link between the Ashton and Bridgewater canals. That included the original offices, and when I first came this way, one had to call in to get a permit to travel the short section – and pay for the privilege, just as boatmen had done a 100 and more years before.

BELOW: The classical offices of the Forth and Clyde Company at Port Dundas, with a range of warehousing beyond lining the quay.

Toll houses

Tolls were levied on all boats in the working days and calculating how much to charge was a complex business, with rates varying with the weight of cargo, the type of goods being carried and the distance travelled. The original Act for the Grand Junction, for example, set a rate of one farthing per ton per mile carried but the rate went up to three farthings for coal and coke. The weight was determined by gauging. Each boat had markings that indicated the height above the water for different weights of cargo. The toll collector had a gauging rod that was set against the boat to measure off that height – and that gave the weight for that particular craft. There was something of a little game played between boatman and toll assessor. The boatman might nonchalantly lean on one side of the vessel to affect the measurement or try to secrete valuable cargo that carried a higher tariff beneath cheaper goods. Looking after tolls was a serious business, and usually the toll collector had a specially designed house that was both home and office.

Toll houses were not a new concept: many had already been built for the turnpike roads that were developed earlier in the 18th century. The normal form was a simple cottage with a prominent bay for the office, specifically designed so that the collector had a clear view both up and down the road.

BELOW: This little toll house of 1783 stands at the Birmingham end of the Birmingham and Fazeley Canal.

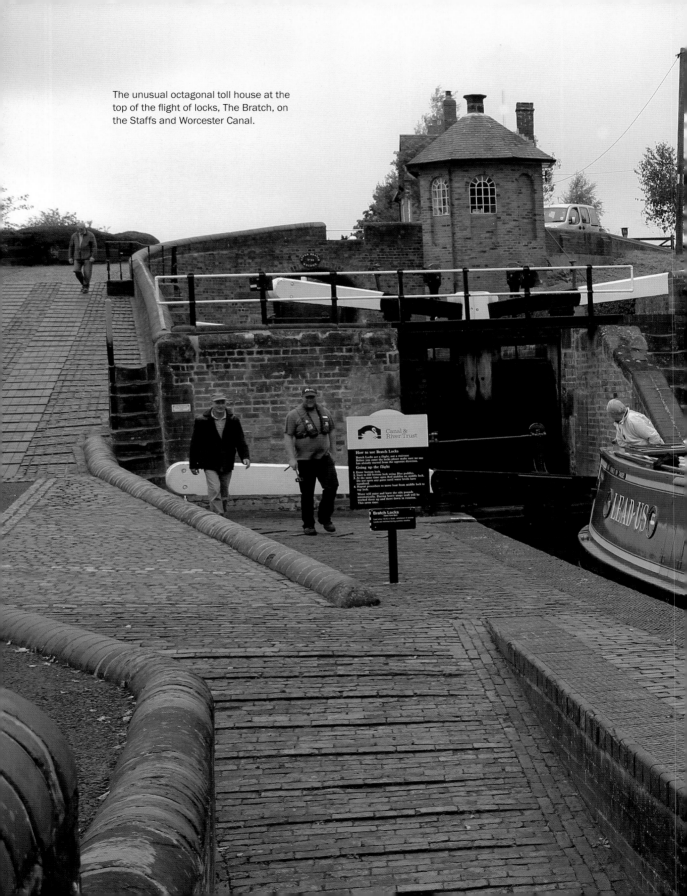

The unusual octagonal toll house at the top of the flight of locks, The Bratch, on the Staffs and Worcester Canal.

Most canal toll houses followed a similar design, and the one at the top of the Farmers Bridge flight of locks, where the Birmingham and Fazeley Canal meets the Birmingham, is a typical example. By contrast, the toll house at the junction of the Worcester and Birmingham and Stratford canals at King's Norton is grander than most, having two storeys instead of the usual one. It is too big and grand to have been used for just toll collection. The oddest can be seen on the Staffs and Worcester at The Bratch. This is an octagonal building, with recessed round-headed windows, and the whole building is topped by a conical roof. At the Stourport end of the same canal, the toll house is conventional in plan but with a prominent gable over the bay and a tall chimney, giving it the appearance of a lodge to some gentleman's estate. It is always pleasant to find that what are essentially practical buildings can be given a slightly quirky appearance.

When Telford built the new main line of the Birmingham Canal, he built it to far wider dimensions than the old Brindley line. As a result, the engineer could design houses that sat on islands in the middle of the canal, so that boats could be gauged on either side and there would be a minimum obstruction to traffic. But it was not always necessary to have special toll houses and on some canals the toll collection job went to the lock keeper. But wherever the tolls were collected, they were essential – not just for profitability, but also to pay the essential running costs for keeping the canal open for business.

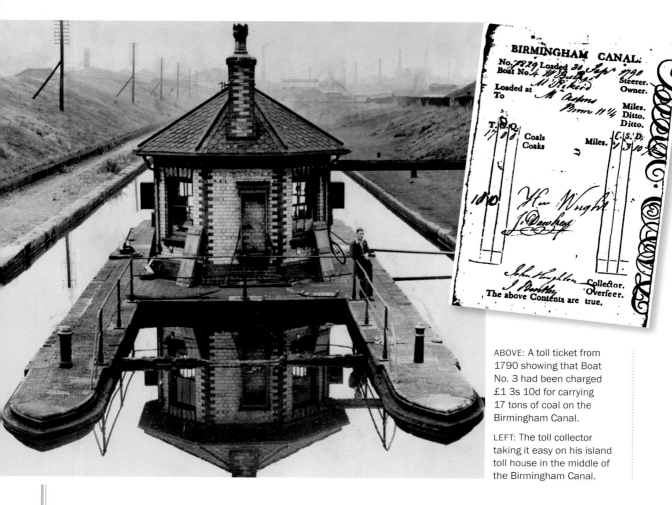

ABOVE: A toll ticket from 1790 showing that Boat No. 3 had been charged £1 3s 10d for carrying 17 tons of coal on the Birmingham Canal.

LEFT: The toll collector taking it easy on his island toll house in the middle of the Birmingham Canal.

Maintenance yards

Many of the structures on the canal were solid and built to last, but others were in need of maintenance. Wooden lock gates did not last for ever, and moveable bridges often needed all or part replaced, for example. This was the work of the maintenance yards, which usually had facilities for working with both timber and metal. So new hinges for lock gates could be made in the forge, virtually the same as the forges of any country blacksmith, while wooden lock gates could be constructed on the premises as well. The maintenance yards were important and that importance can be seen in the fact that many of them looked even grander than the company's office.

Bulbourne Yard, at the northern end of Tring cutting, is typical of many, and actually remained in use as the main centre for making and repairing lock gates for the system right up to 2003. The site consists of individual workshops and cottages for the workforce. There is an extensive wharf area so that heavy material could be moved into and out of boats with the help of manually operated cranes. Inside the workshops, powered machinery was virtually non-existent. The main building is a low, single-storey structure with a shallow pitched roof and boasting a clock tower topped by a pagoda-style roof. In an age when few working men could afford the luxury of a watch, the clock was essential to mark the start and close of the working day.

Considering that maintenance yards are essentially practical workshops, it is surprising to find that they can also be as visually satisfying as grander, architect-designed buildings. Hartshill Yard on the Coventry Canal is an excellent example. Often the effect is born out of necessity. Set back

BELOW: Making wooden lock gates at Bulbourne.

Bulbourne yard on the Grand Union
Canal as a working site, with a
maintenance boat moored alongside.

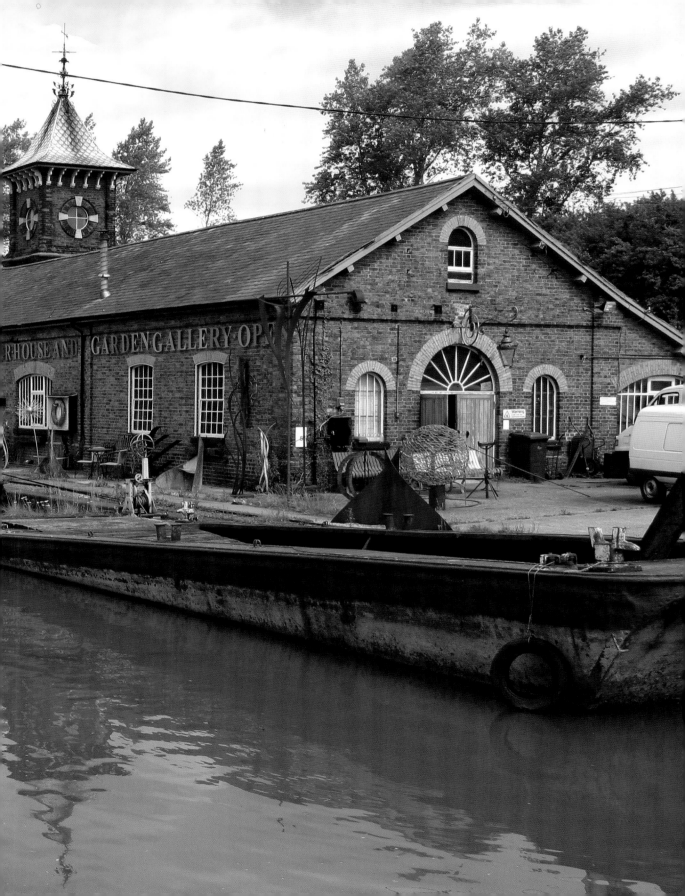

from the main channel, it is approached via a short arm running off at quite a sharp angle. To minimise the potential damage caused by maintenance boats making the awkward turn into the basin, the walls are set in a graceful curve. The building itself has neat architectural flourishes – round-headed windows echoed by blind arches. And like so many buildings of the period, the patina of age has added to the charm.

In general, maintenance yards are situated conveniently on main lines in a central position. In the Birmingham system, however, there are workshops at Bradley that stand at the end of a short branch line, but remained in use manufacturing lock gates. The site seems inappropriate, but it wasn't always like this: Bradley was once on one of the loops off the new main line, but that was severed years ago, leaving the site

isolated. Many of the old yards have been adapted over the years for different purposes. Hillmorton, on the northern section of the Oxford Canal, is a good example. It lies close to the flight of locks and is approached from the canal by a short arm, crossed by a richly hued brick bridge. Beyond that is a basin with the yard workshops. For many years, the main building was home to British Waterways' architecture department, while hire boats were kept in the basin.

One yard is of special interest. It stands at the top of the short flight of locks at Claydon on the Oxford Canal. There are the usual workshops, built of mellow red brick, in an L-shaped plan – one side

BELOW: Hartshill maintenance yard on the Coventry Canal. The squat chimney indicates that, among other facilities, there was a forge for ironwork.

ABOVE: The basin at Hillmorton on the Oxford Canal has gone through a variety of different uses, as a maintenance yard and later as home to the British Waterways architecture department and hire boat base.

for the forge, the other for woodworking. What is unusual is that there is also an extensive wharf and canal-side stabling. Few companies ran their own fleets of boats and other boat owners were expected to make their own arrangements. The arrangements could be quite crude. At Falling Sands near Kidderminster on the Staffs and Worcester, the canal runs below sandstone cliffs, where caves have been utilised for stabling. One company that did run its own fleet was the Shropshire Union.

The Shropshire Union was, as the name suggests, formed from an amalgamation of various canals, one of which was the Chester. This was an early canal, completed in 1779, originally planned to join the Dee at Chester to the Trent and Mersey via the Middlewich Branch, but later extended to Nantwich. It has a spectacular start after leaving the river at Chester, where it hugs the city walls like a medieval moat.

With the arrival of the Birmingham and Liverpool Junction, it acquired new importance as a vital link between Birmingham and the Mersey at Ellesmere Port. As a result, a lot of new building work was

put in hand. Bunbury was already an important spot with a double lock, lock cottage and wharf. Now a spacious stable block was added. The buildings are handsome and are notable for the cowls on the roof, ensuring good ventilation. Canal horses had to be sturdy beasts but here they were particularly well cared for, and the company even paid for a vet to keep them in good condition. Port Dundas, mentioned above, not only has an exceptionally grand office building but also boasts equally imposing stables. Their overall design is in fact similar to that for the offices, with the central pediment bay.

Apart from the obvious devices needed to make the canal work, the companies were often required under the terms of their Acts to provide a certain amount of canal furniture, most commonly distance posts. These had been made compulsory

An interesting complex at Bunbury on the Chester Canal, with stables and a small office to the right of the double locks and just a glimpse of the lock cottage to the left.

for the new turnpike roads and now they were also needed on the canals. They were essential in establishing distances travelled, as tolls were calculated on that basis and the posts were the only agreed marks in the absence of annotated maps. They come in a great variety of different forms. On many canals they are simply carved stone slabs with the minimum of information, while others are more elaborate. Some are quite crudely carved; others are testimony to the craftsmanship of anonymous masons. Some milestones came complete with the names of the two termini and the distances between them. So, the same two names would be carved afresh for each stone. An alternative was to use cast iron. The same basic mould could be used over and over again, and the only changes would be to alter the numerals each time for a new casting. The Trent and Mersey mileposts are particularly complex, with double tops – one slanted towards one named terminus, the other facing the opposite way. It is quite surprising to find just what variety there is. But if officialdom provided an interesting array of building and artefacts, the commercial companies that used the canal brought even more diversity.

ABOVE: A cast iron milepost from the Grand Junction Canal days, before it was absorbed into the larger Grand Union system.

BELOW: An elaborate Shropshire Union milepost.

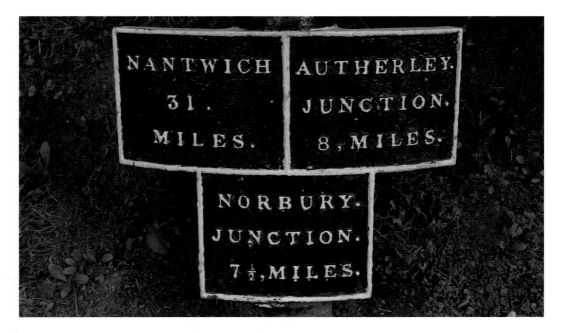

SETTING UP OFFICE

The following instructions for setting up new offices were for the Warwick and Birmingham Canal:

• To put a skirting board round the Room appointed to the use of the Committee and to put a hearth stone and chimney piece for the same.

• To build a brewhouse, privy and wall to make the yard and garden private and entire – to sink a well and put down a pump – to glaze the windows in the room to be occupied as an office.

With offices in place, clerks needed to be employed and the Kennet and Avon engineer John Rennie laid down the requirements:

• 'Clerks should be chosen who are not just capable of keeping books; the ideal should also be capable of purchasing the land and agreeing for damages, settling the situation for accommodation, etc, etc – in this way I think his time will be fully employed.'

BELOW: Originally, locks would have been identified by painted numbers, mostly replaced by cast iron number plates.

PLACES TO VISIT

CLEVELAND HOUSE: original offices of Kennet and Avon Company, above Cleveland tunnel, Sydney Road, Bath BA2 6NR.

BEECH HOUSE: original offices of Ellesmere Canal Company, Ellesmere SY12 0AA.

TOLL HOUSE: Staffs NS Worcester, The Bratch, Wombourne WV5 8DW.

BULBOURNE MAINTENANCE YARD: Grand Union Canal, Tring HP23 5QF.

CHAPTER 8

WHARFS, WAREHOUSES AND BASINS

Once a canal was finished, its advantages were obvious to all the communities on or near its banks, from hamlets and villages to towns and city centres. Small communities only needed the most basic facilities. For some small villages, all that was needed was a simple wharf, an area of flattened land, usually with a cobbled surface and stone coping, with perhaps one or two mooring rings for boats to tie up. Such an area can be seen next to the church at Shipton-on-Cherwell. Nearby Lower Heyford is scarcely larger but has a far more extensive wharf with a small warehouse. It has been much altered over the years and is now home to a large boat hire company, but it remains an impressive example of the trouble and expense that small communities felt were worthwhile. Thanks to such facilities, rural communities could enjoy the luxury of coal fires. Now the coal could be brought from the Midlands from the Coventry Canal to their wharf on the Oxford.

Urban warehouses

Towns necessarily had more extensive facilities. Simple hand cranes were often erected and warehouses built to store goods in transit. At Skipton, there is an extensive wharf area beside the Leeds and Liverpool Canal and a grand warehouse, with covered hoists to move goods up and down the multi-storeyed building. But the canal also provided special facilities for the stone quarries outside the town. The Springs Branch leaves the main line and heads off under the shadow of the castle to a special wharf where the stone could be loaded.

Several carrying companies arranged and paid for their own warehousing. Pickford's had

LEFT: Lower Heyford is only a village, but still has an extensive wharf and warehouse on the Oxford Canal, now used as a base for hire boats.

begun trading as a road haulage firm, but quickly recognised the superiority of canals and ran an extensive fleet of narrow boats. They originally had an extensive complex of warehouses and wharfs at City Road basin at Islington on the Regent's Canal. The basin has survived but there is little else to remind us of the carrying firm: happily, the same is not true of other parts of their watery network. At Worksop on the Chesterfield Canal, they built a warehouse with an arch straddling the waterway. Boats could be moored beneath the arch and goods could be hauled up through a trapdoor. Everything could be kept dry, regardless of the weather.

LEFT: Pickford's had an extensive fleet of narrow boats, with depots all over the country. Their warehouse at Worksop on the Chesterfield Canal was built out over the canal, so that boats could be unloaded via a trapdoor in the arch.

BELOW: Burnley was a major centre for the cotton industry and as a consequence required suitably large warehouses. Protection is provided by the extensive canopy and covered hoists carried goods to the upper storeys.

An alternative way of keeping goods dry can be seen beside the Marple locks on the Peak Forest Canal. Samuel Oldknow was an industrialist who transformed the region in the late 18th century by building textile mills and he was one of the main promoters of the canal. This was his own warehouse, built beside the canal with an arch at one side that allowed vessels to float right inside the building. The bigger the town, the grander the buildings, and this was especially true of the industrial towns of northern England. At Blackburn, at the heart of the burgeoning cotton industry, there is a splendid warehouse. It is built alongside an extensive wharf but has a canopy reaching right out over the water under which boats could shelter. It stands three storeys high and two covered hoists rise above the canopy to transfer goods to the upper floors.

The most famous wharf in an industrial area has to be Wigan Pier, which does exist but is very modest, little more than a paved area, used at one time for passenger boats. However, the town does also have a warehouse complex very similar to that at Blackburn.

Canal/river junctions

There are some areas where extensive development was inevitable. Junctions always have a special significance but are especially important where transhipment is necessary – for example, when transferring goods between narrow boats and wide barges. This happened when the narrow boats of the Staffs and Worcester Canal joined the River Severn, which in those days was served by large sailing barges, the Severn trows.

There was some debate as to where the junction should be made. A number of canal histories tell the story that Brindley wanted to meet the river at the then thriving inland port of Bewdley. However, the town's residents wanted none of it, sourly referring to the canal as a 'stinking ditch'. Nothing could be further from the truth. The town actually petitioned Parliament to bring the canal there, welcoming the increase in trade and fearing a powerful competitor if it didn't arrive. Their fears were justified. Brindley looked at the lie of the land and decided he would have far less trouble and save on engineering works if he followed the valley of the River Stour. His route ended at a spot by the river graced by a solitary inn, but it would grow rapidly and become the town of Stourport.

The first stage of development involved the construction of a large canal basin, immediately north of the mouth of the Stour. Because the Severn is prone to flooding, it was built with an entrance 29 feet (9m) above the normal level of the river. The basin was joined to the river by a broad lock able to take vessels up to 75 feet (23m) long with a 15-foot (4.6m) beam, which meant it could be used both by narrow boats and the trows. There was a toll house for collecting revenue and a narrow lock at the far side of the basin gave access to the canal.

The scheme was a huge success. Trade to Stourport grew rapidly – and, as they feared, the citizens of Bewdley found their trade diminishing. A major development programme was begun at Stourport in 1771. A new basin was added to the

west of the original and then two more intermediate basins were added. They were connected by locks: two barge locks and four narrow locks for canal boats. The latter locks were built as risers, in effect two-lock staircases. A warehouse was added – a long, ten-bay brick building, undistinguished apart from an ornate clock tower in the centre of the roof. The canal company recognised that they would have to supply accommodation for merchants and traders, so they built the large, elegant Tontine Hotel in 1772. Constructed of red brick with a Welsh slate roof, the most striking features are the Venetian windows to either side of the main entrance – the porch is a later addition. The hotel also had an extensive stable block, now converted into housing. The town developed rapidly and the area immediately around the basins has a wealth of fine Georgian houses. Stourport is in fact a Georgian new town that owes its existence entirely to the arrival of the canal. It is not the only example of a canal new town.

Stourport was developed at the start of the canal age: Ellesmere Port came at the end. When the Ellesmere Canal was built, part of it consisted of an extension of the old Chester Canal northwards to the Mersey. The spot where canal and river joined was named after the canal but initially there was not very much development, apart from a lock and basin. The situation changed with the construction of the Birmingham and Liverpool Junction Canal. Traffic increased dramatically and a whole new complex of warehouses was developed by Thomas Telford.

When it was built, the port area contained the largest array of warehousing to be found on the waterways. All the warehouses were designed with boat holes for loading under cover, and the work of the docks was improved over the years. Hydraulic power was introduced to work cranes and capstans in 1873. The pump house contains two steam engines built by the Armstrong works, who also provided the hydraulic machinery. Sadly, many of the original warehouses were destroyed by a fire, but enough remains to give an excellent idea of just how important the whole complex was, and it is now home to one section of the

National Waterways Museum. The town grew up round the basin, and the arrival of an even greater waterway, the Manchester Ship Canal, increased its importance. It developed as a major industrial centre – but it all began with a lock and a basin.

Shardlow stands at the junction of the River Trent and the Trent and Mersey Canal. It was not quite a new town in the same way as Stourport was, as there had been a small settlement here since medieval times, but it changed and developed rapidly with the arrival of the canal. One can see the effect everywhere in the wealth of new buildings that arrived following the completion of the waterway. There are many fine Georgian houses, suggesting that trade had brought prosperity to the area, but the other indicator lies on the purely utilitarian buildings. Warehouses show a wealth of interesting detail. One warehouse is notable for an array of semicircular windows with cast iron frames. Such frames could be ordered ready-made, and ones similar to these can be seen in the contemporary catalogue of the Andrew Handyside

ABOVE: Ellesmere Port developed at the junction of what is now the Shropshire Union and the Mersey Canal. It could be accessed through the narrow lock for canal boats or the broad lock for barges.

Foundry of Derby. Although built to take goods carried by water, goods stored there could also be moved by land. Another warehouse has a rounded corner next to the road, known as a waggon corner for a good reason: if a careless carter knocked his vehicle against the edge, it would slide off the curve instead of knocking lumps off the brickwork. The most striking building is Trent Corn Mill No.2 of 1780. The date is significant because this is just three years after completion of the canal, and some entrepreneur thought it worthwhile to spend a good deal of money on what was, for the time, a very large grain mill. There are the usual hoists on the land side, but on the canal side there is a pediment bay with a large arched opening at water level to allow boats inside the building.

The large warehouse at Stourport
is known as the Clock Warehouse
for obvious reasons.

TOP: The complex at Ellesmere Port was designed by Thomas Telford. Sadly, many of the original buildings were destroyed in a fire, but it remains an important canal centre and home to one section of the National Waterways Museum.

ABOVE: For many commodities carried by canal, it was advisable to load and unload in the dry. This warehouse at Chester has 'boat holes' – the boats could be run in through the arches.

RIGHT: Shardlow developed rapidly, with the completion of the Trent and Mersey Canal, as the point where canal and river boats exchanged goods. A new grain mill was built with a large boat hole.

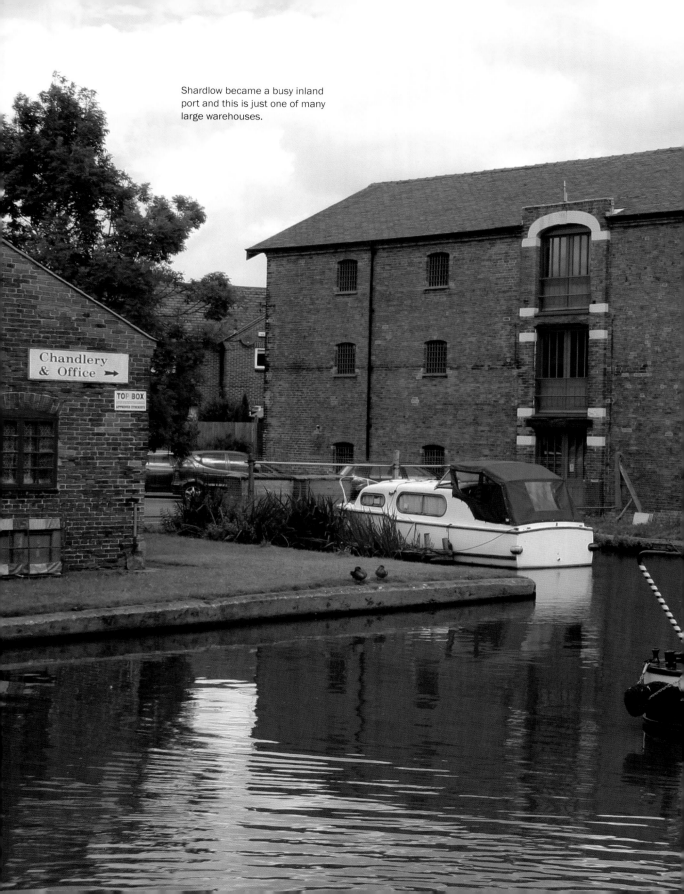

Shardlow became a busy inland port and this is just one of many large warehouses.

Another important junction can be found where the Regent's Canal meets the Thames at Limehouse Basin. Nowhere in the system has seen quite so many changes as there have been here. Changes were constantly being made to the plans even before it was opened in 1820: at first there was to be one small dock, then it was decided to have two docks – one large ship dock and a smaller barge dock. The final scheme opted for a single dock, with a wide entrance lock to the tidal river and a smaller canal lock on the opposite side of the basin. Originally it was planned with sloping stone sides and wooden jetties, then a more conventional straight-sided version was built. Facilities were at first limited – there was not even a crane on site until 1822. But over the years it prospered and there was a busy trade, with coasters coming in off the tidal river to be unloaded into a fleet of narrow boats. It reached its heyday in the 1930s, but in the second half of the 20th century there was a steady decline. Ships no longer berthed in the Pool of London but were moored downstream at the more extensive deep-water docks at Tilbury.

Today, almost nothing of the old Limehouse remains. Instead of trading vessels, there is now a marina for pleasure craft. The old warehouses have all gone and in their place are blocks of flats that are less than inspiring. The ship dock has also gone and a new smaller lock, to take vessels 100 foot by 30 foot (30m x 9m), was built inside the chamber of the old in 1989. The one gain has been the attractive new control tower at the entrance. If nothing else, Limehouse makes one appreciate the almost effortless graceful simplicity of the often anonymous builders of 200 years ago.

Ship canals offer a special case. The Scottish canals, Crinan and Caledonian, were built as short cuts to avoid lengthy detours around the Kintyre peninsula in the first case and the north of Scotland in the other, and were largely used

RIGHT: Limehouse Basin, where the Regent's Canal joins the Thames, was once a thriving commercial dock. Today it is home to pleasure boats and surrounded by new developments.

LEFT: When looking at canal basins, it is easy to underestimate the amount of work needed for their construction. This photograph shows the construction of a basin on the Rochdale Canal in Manchester.

BELOW: The basin where the Crinan ship canal meets the sea. *The Duke of Normandy II* is a tug built in 1934.

BOTTOM RIGHT: Gloucester docks, at the northern end of the Gloucester and Sharpness Canal, has a wealth of 19th-century warehouses.

by fishing vessels, so there was little need for extensive wharfs and warehouses, though the basin at Crinan itself is one of the most charming spots on the system.

The Gloucester and Sharpness, however, is very different, with major inland ports at both ends. As at Limehouse, there have been great changes over the years, but here they have not had such a disastrous effect on the canal scene. The canal leaves the Severn at Gloucester and opens immediately out into the dock area. This was extensively rebuilt in the 19th century, with multi-storey brick warehouses. They are an impressive sight, but much of their attraction lies in the detail, in contrasts in texture and form. The brickwork has mellowed with the years and forms a rich background to the timber of hoists and the iron of tie beams. There is a reminder that this was once regularly visited by seagoing vessels in the Mariners Church, a small, rather plain Victorian building almost overwhelmed by its commercial neighbours but still in use. The warehouses have been adapted to a variety of different uses and one now houses the National Waterways Museum, the partner to the Ellesmere Port museum. The whole

scene is enlivened by the variety of craft out on the water, including a steam-powered dredger. There is still a working boatyard here, specialising in restoring and rigging traditional craft. Tall ships are regular visitors and today the docks are one of the city's most popular attractions.

Originally, the plan was to have the southern end of the canal at Berkeley Pill, but the plans were changed in favour of a new dock at Sharpness. This is almost unique in that it is still a thriving inland canal port. The facilities were modernised in the 19th century at the same time as the improvements were being made at Gloucester. The lock down to the tidal Severn was constructed in 1874 to accommodate the larger vessels coming up the river. It is a massive affair, 320 feet (98m) long and 52 feet (15m) wide. It gives access to the large basin with its mixture of old and new buildings. The 19th-century warehouses are virtually identical to those at Gloucester, but where in the latter they dominate the scene, here they are overwhelmed noticeably by the immense 20th-century grain elevator. Where Gloucester docks are now largely devoted to tourism and shopping, Sharpness remains very much a working site.

The Gloucester warehouses have found a variety of new uses, including this one now housing an excellent canal museum.

Canal/canal junctions

On occasions, even a junction between two canals can create problems. The original Birmingham Canal ended near Broad Street in Birmingham and was later joined by the Worcester and Birmingham. But the Birmingham company were concerned that the newcomer would drain off water from their canal to serve the flight of locks leading up to the junction. They insisted on a physical barrier between the two canals – the Worcester Bar. As a result, although both canals could be used by the same narrow boats, there was no through route and cargoes had to be shipped from boats on one side of the barrier to similar boats on the other side. This, of course, required a basin, where boats could wait, and warehousing – hence Gas Street Basin. Later, the water problem was solved in a more sensible manner by the introduction of a shallow stop lock.

Gas Street was once one of Birmingham's best kept secrets. Road access was via steps, hidden away behind a high brick wall; the only clue to what lay behind was a red hatch in the wall. This could be opened up by the fire brigade, who could use the water in the basin for their hoses in an emergency. The basin itself was, like many others, surrounded by old warehouses and home to narrow boats, many used as homes. There were toll houses on either side of the stop lock. Then, half a century ago, it was decided to demolish the warehouses and for years the site was left bare and forlorn. The boat owners no longer had their snug little enclave, but were overlooked by the bare spaces of a featureless temporary car park. However, there had already been a development scheme at nearby Cambrian Wharf, which had demonstrated how, by sympathetic treatment,

BELOW: Older buildings have survived on the Worcester and Birmingham Canal by the entrance to Gas Street Basin, Birmingham.

ABOVE: Gas Street has now developed into a popular city venue, but is still home to narrow boats.

old buildings could be brought back into use and a wharf could become an attractive place to visit. A new pub helped to attract visitors. After years of neglect, development got under way, transforming Gas Street. Today, the old toll house by the lock is still there and narrow boats are still moored, but the surroundings have been changed completely, turning this once peaceful spot into a bustling area of bars, pubs and restaurants. Visitors can decide for themselves whether a scheme based on redeveloping the historic buildings would have provided a more characterful area than one based on demolition and new build.

Canal termini

Some canals built to serve towns and cities finish up at a dead end, an obvious site for a basin. One such terminus can be found near the centre of Coventry. This is an attractive site, approached from the road via the old wharfinger's office, a simple brick building with a pyramidal roof. Beyond it is the wide basin with a cobbled yard and a peninsula to provide an extra length of wharf. The whole is dominated by the warehouse at the end, which was added in the 1830s and is very much of its time. The roof has been extended over the wharf to create a canopy carried on cast iron pillars. Wooden hoists rise above the canopy to serve the upper floors. Until recently the rest of the site was empty but it has now been developed, with buildings that are in sympathy with the old. On the wharf is a statue of James Brindley inspecting his canal plans. One suspects he might have approved.

While the Coventry Canal dates back to the Brindley years, work on the Sheffield Canal was only authorised in 1815 and became part of the wider Sheffield and South Yorkshire Navigation. The terminus is full of interest. At the end of the basin is what is known as the 'Straddle' warehouse, so called because it does literally straddle the water to allow boats underneath. There is an impressive grain warehouse on a very grand scale that was mainly used to house barley for local breweries. Judging by its size, the citizens of Sheffield are a thirsty lot. It has both arches for boats and a canopied wharf. The old dry dock has been restored, with the entrance crossed by a swing bridge. The original buildings have all found new uses: the Straddle warehouse as offices, the grain warehouse as apartments. It is one of the most successful schemes for renewal of urban canal spaces.

The buildings and wharfs that still dot our canal system are a never-ending source of variety and interest. Some were built by the canal companies themselves. For example, the small basin at Ellesmere, a market town whose main 'industry' was making Cheshire cheese, has a Shropshire Union Company warehouse that carried a sign proudly announcing that they could carry goods to destinations throughout England and Wales. By contrast, many of the warehouses on the Forth and Clyde Canal were built by distillers to hold either grain or barrels full of whisky. They are all a vital part of the canal heritage, and it is to be hoped that, in future, developers will find ways of adapting them for new uses, rather than demolishing them and replacing them with modern buildings that experience suggests will seldom be as interesting as the old.

RIGHT: The Straddle warehouse really does straddle the canal at the city end of Sheffield Basin.

BELOW: A statue of James Brindley looks out over Coventry Basin, which has been sympathetically developed.

PICKFORDS

The Penny Magazine of 1842 gave a picture of the scene at one of the country's busiest wharfs: Pickford's on the Regent's Canal.

'At the wharf of Messrs. Pickford and Co., in the City Road, can be witnessed, on a larger scale than at any other part of the kingdom, the general operations connected with canal traffic.

This large establishment nearly surrounds the southern extremity of the City Road Basin. From the coach-road we can see little of the premises; but on passing to a street in the rear we come to a pair of large folding gates opening into an area or court, and we cannot remain here many minutes especially in the morning or evening, without witnessing a scene of astonishing activity. From about five or six o'clock in the evening waggons are pouring in from various parts of town, laden with goods intended to be sent into the country per canal. In the morning, on the other hand, laden waggons are leaving the establishment, conveying to different parts of the metropolis goods which have arrived per canal during the night.'

PLACES TO VISIT

NATIONAL WATERWAYS MUSEUM, Shropshire Union Canal, South Pier Road, Ellesmere Port CH65 4FW.

GLOUCESTER DOCKS, Gloucester and Sharpness Canal, Southgate Street, Gloucester GL1 2EH.

SHEFFIELD BASIN, Sheffield Canal, Victoria Quays, Sheffield S2 5SYOK.

PORT DUNDAS, WHARF, FORTH AND CLYDE CANAL, PORT DUNDAS, Glasgow G4 9TB.

Portland Basin stands at the junction of two restored canals – the Huddersfield Narrow and the Peak Forest.

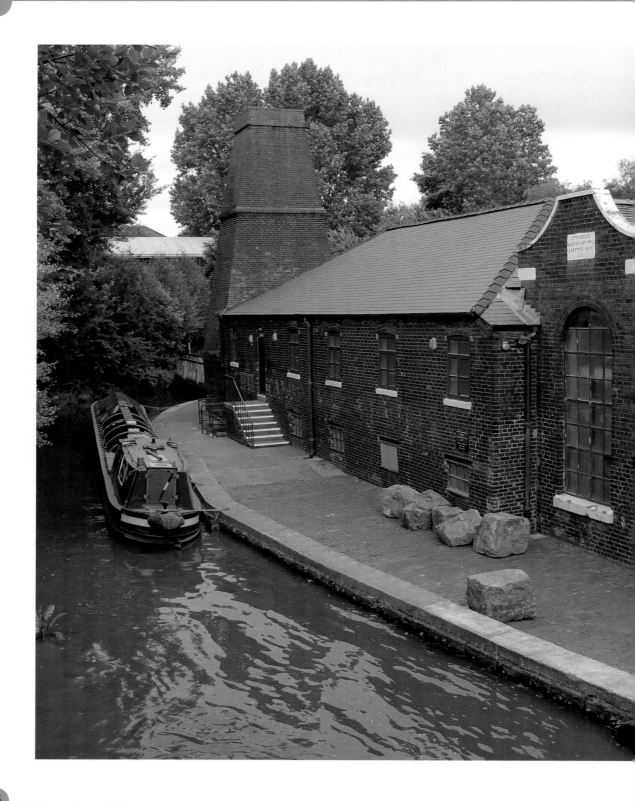

CHAPTER 9

THE INDUSTRIAL WORLD

The Bridgewater Canal was constructed to serve the coal-mining industry, and coal had a vital part to play in developing trade on the canals. But it was not only mine owners who saw the advantages of water transport. The success of the Bridgewater encouraged other industrialists to promote canals to serve their concerns.

The potteries

It was the great potter Josiah Wedgwood who was the driving force behind the Trent and Mersey Canal, the first major route to be promoted after the opening of the Bridgewater. He had been working on developing a new type of pottery, which was creamy white in colour. Up to then the local earthenware had either been a basic light brown or, if white was needed, was covered by a heavy glaze. Wedgwood was looking to produce more elegant ware to appeal to an aristocratic market. He wanted to import a lighter clay from the West Country, which could then be further lightened in tone by being mixed with powdered flint before firing. So he needed to bring in material from both the east and west of England – and he needed

LEFT: Bone and flint were used to lighten the colour of the local clays for use in the potteries and they were ground in the Etruscan Mill at the junction of the Trent and Mersey and Caldon canals.

to send the finished ware to the customers and especially to new showrooms he was opening in London.

The clay could be brought by ship up the west coast to Liverpool and the Mersey; the flint would be shipped from East Anglia to the Trent. A canal joining the two rivers was exactly what he needed. He was an assiduous promoter of the Trent and Mersey company and was to become its treasurer – a post that he wryly noted paid '£00 per annum out of which he bear his own expenses'. The chief engineer was, inevitably, James Brindley, at £200 a year. Work got under way as soon as the Act was passed in 1766. Wedgwood at once began planning a new factory to be built alongside the canal, together with some houses for the workforce. He also planned for a new house for his family on the opposite side of the canal. He had been inspired by ancient pottery that he believed, erroneously as it turned out, to be Etruscan, so he named the whole complex Etruria.

The Wedgwood works were later moved to a more modern factory at Barlaston and little

ABOVE: This 18th-century enamelled plaque shows the Trent and Mersey Canal shortly after opening, with Josiah Wedgwood's home, Etruria Hall.

now remains of the original works. One surviving structure is a small circular building with a domed roof that was once the workshop for the modellers, who made the original pots that would later be reproduced in large numbers. Wedgwood's home, Etruria Hall, however, is still there, but is now a hotel. Wedgwood had a vision of the canal sweeping past his new home in a gracious curve, but Brindley would have none of it, so the potter had to make do with a straight stretch of water between house and works. The building itself is in the typical neoclassical style of the period, but is not a very distinguished example. Other potteries soon followed to take advantage of the canal; Middleport is a good example. There is an extensive wharf, with a small hand crane next to

the packing house. As soon as the ceramics had been crated up for transport, they could be loaded straight on to the waiting boat. The pottery is open to visitors.

It was not just the potteries themselves that took advantage of the canal. The flints from East Anglia had to be treated before use. First, they had to be calcined, heated in a kiln to make them more brittle, and then ground into a powder. Later it was discovered that crushed animal bones could also be used – hence bone china. The Etruscan Bone and Flint Mill was first established on a site at the

junction of the Trent and Mersey and Caldon canals in 1857. The most prominent feature of the main building is a tall pyramidal structure, the calcining kiln. It was in this that the flints were heated – a process that required a ton of coal for each hundredweight of flint, so regular coal deliveries to the wharf were essential. Inside the main building is the crusher, powered by a small horizontal steam engine. The site is now an industrial museum.

The Caldon Canal was originally built to serve the limestone quarries of Caldon Low. But it too was to become home to a flint mill, at Cheddleton. There had been a grain mill on a nearby site for many years, and with the arrival of the canal it was converted to flint grinding and a second mill added. Everything is ordered to make the most efficient use of water transport. The mills are powered by waterwheels turned by the River Churnet. The canal itself passes at a higher level than the river, and the difference is taken advantage of, so the wharf is built up from river level to canal level. Boats unloaded the raw material on to the very substantial stone wharf. There are two kilns built directly into the wharf, so that coal and flint can be shovelled straight into the top of the kiln once they have been unloaded. The calcined flint is then shovelled out from openings at the foot of the kiln and taken by railed track to the mills for grinding. The actual grinding is carried out by heavy stones mounted on sweep arms, continuously circling and powered by the waterwheels. Like the other flint mill, this too is open to the public.

Textile mills

If one industry was crucial to the development of the Industrial Revolution it was textiles, in particular cotton spinning. Sir Richard Arkwright developed machinery for spinning cotton that could be powered by a waterwheel and developed his first mill at Cromford in Derbyshire in 1771. By 1780 he felt the need to improve communications and promoted the Cromford Canal. It is a measure of the importance he attached to the enterprise that it was thought to be worth constructing a canal, which had major engineering works. Within its 14½ mile (23km) length there were three tunnels – two quite short, but Butterley tunnel was 3,083 yards (2,819m) long – and there were also two major aqueducts over rivers. It linked Cromford to the Nottingham coalfield, as well as providing a route for the raw cotton and spun yarn. Coal was not needed in great quantities in the industry in the early days, except for such comparatively mundane operations as heating water for dye works and similar tasks. All that changed dramatically, however, with the arrival of the Boulton and Watt steam engine, developed to work machinery.

Because the first textile mills were all worked by waterwheels, they had to be sited where there was a suitable supply of water. Also, in those years, the mills produced yarn only: cloth was still woven in cottages on hand looms. But by the end of the 18th century, mills were being developed in which all the processes were mechanised. At first, advances all took place in the cotton industry, but later spread to woollens. The change meant that mills could be built almost anywhere, and industrialists rapidly came to see that being alongside a first-class transport route was a huge advantage. The industrial landscape began to change – and canals were at the heart of the changes.

One town illustrating the changes that followed the coming of canals is Hebden Bridge on the Rochdale Canal. Wool had been spun and woven in the region for centuries; however, the heart of the industry was not down in the valley but in the hilltop village of Heptonstall, overlooking the town and joined to it by an old packhorse route. In these early days, it was a cottage industry, with women carding and spinning the wool, while men worked at the looms. When the new technology appeared, the focus shifted from wool to cotton and from handcrafts to steam-powered mills. They needed to bring in the raw cotton imported from America into Liverpool and required huge quantities of coal for the boilers to feed the engines. The old hilltop village was no longer appropriate and development switched to the valley and the area round the canal. Hebden Bridge, once subservient to Heptonstall, grew rapidly and soon mills were lining the canal and the town acquired an extensive wharf. There was a problem, however – finding space to house the growing workforce. In many mill towns, the answer was found in back-to-back housing, but here the town climbs the steep hill. The solution was what might be called 'top-to-bottom' houses. Looking up at the terraces, they appear to be conventional; however, close inspection shows that the side facing the canal appears to have four-storey houses but, if you go up a level to the street, the houses appear to be two-storey. This is because one row is built on top of the other, so the front doors for one row of houses are on the lower level, while the front doors for the rest are facing onto the street above.

There are cruises available from the wharf and the impact of the canal in creating a thriving industrial centre soon becomes obvious, with mills lining the route.

TOP LEFT: The wharf at Cheddleton flint mill on the Caldon Canal. In the foreground can be seen the openings of the tops of the kilns into which the flints were loaded for calcining.

BOTTOM LEFT: One of a pair of water-powered flint mills at Cheddleton.

OVERLEAF: When the Rochdale Canal arrived at Hebden Bridge, industrialists at once began building new textile mills alongside the waterway to take advantage of the improved transport it offered.

It was not just in existing industrial areas that the arrival of a canal gave an impetus to development. Skipton was a thriving market town when the Leeds and Liverpool arrived. Soon a new area was developed with cotton mills and new housing. The seemingly haphazard nature of the old town gave way to regimented rows of terraced houses, typical of other mill towns but an alien presence in Skipton. The industrial landscape is seen at its most intense at the Lancashire end of the canal. Much of that industry has now gone. The writer and biographer L.T.C. Rolt once described the view from the Burnley 'Straight Mile', the huge embankment that towers over the town, as being the finest industrial landscape in Britain. Not any more: much of the old has been swept away. But at the southern end of the bank, by the old canal maintenance yard, the waterway makes a sharp turn and enters a very different world. Here, mills and houses jostle for space. Most of the development happened at the end of the 18th and beginning of the 19th centuries and tall chimneys thrust above the rooftops tell us that these all relied on steam power. Some are easier than others to date – Trafalgar Mill, for example, was clearly named shortly after the famous naval battle.

RIGHT: Skipton was a traditional market town until the arrival of the Leeds and Liverpool Canal brought the textile mills to its banks.

LEFT: Blackburn is famous as a cotton town, but Daisyfield Mill, built in 1870 beside the Leeds and Liverpool Canal, is a massive, steam-powered grain mill.

ABOVE: The Leeds and Liverpool Canal winding between the cotton mills of Burnley. Since this photo was taken many mills have been demolished.

TOP: The Trencherfield Mill engine: the ropes round the flywheel took the drive to every floor of the mill. Supplying the monster with coal kept the canal boats busy.

BOTTOM: Trencherfield Mill at Wigan is close to the famous Wigan Pier and home to a magnificent mill steam engine.

To get a better understanding of the close connection between the transport system and the voracious appetite for fuel for the mill engines, there is no better place to visit than Wigan. Trencherfield Mill by the canal contains one of the most powerful surviving mill engines, and although it no longer works machinery, it is regularly steamed for visitors. The first mill engines were beam engines, working at low pressure. Later engines were built with horizontal cylinders, providing direct drive via a simple crank and steamed at ever higher pressures. They were still being built and installed as recently as the early years of the 20th century. The Trencherfield engine began work in 1907 and is a monster. Steam pressure had risen to 200 pounds per square inch, and that was so high that the exhaust steam was still under pressure when it left the cylinder. Rather than waste that energy, it was then passed into a second intermediate cylinder, but even then it was not exhausted and went to a third, low-pressure cylinder – hence the name of 'triple expansion engine' for this type of machine. The drive turns an immense flywheel, 26 feet (8m) in diameter. Grooves round the rim hold 54 ropes, which transmit the drive to

every floor of the mill. And just as a 19th-century mill would have done, to keep the works going depended on the coal delivered to the mill wharf.

All the canals of the north of England have mills along their banks, many of which are very impressive. But the cotton industry extended further south as well. A water-powered mill for spinning cotton and printing calico was built beside the Birmingham and Fazeley Canal at Fazeley in 1790. It was part of an estate bought by Sir Robert Peel, after which it became known as Peel Mill. It prospered: originally three storeys high and eight bays wide, it was later extended to 19 bays. Like most 18th-century cotton mills, it was quite narrow, built to fit snugly round the spinning machines of the day. The tall chimney indicates that the mill was later converted to steam power. Another splendid textile mill with a site chosen alongside a canal is Ebley Mill on the Stroudwater Canal. Built in 1818 and extended in the 1860s, this is an unusually attractive structure, built of local limestone in a style vaguely reminiscent of a French chateau. The former woollen mill has been sensitively restored and now houses local council offices. The canal too has recently been brought back to life and the mill can be admired in its original setting.

The most striking example of a canal-side textile development has to be Saltaire beside the Leeds and Liverpool Canal. Sir Titus Salt was an industrialist who had in his time been an important citizen of Bradford, as both alderman and mayor. He had also built up a business as a wool spinner and manufacturer, but in Liverpool he came across some bales of alpaca in which no one showed any interest. He found that, when spun, it produced a most attractive soft cloth. He decided he needed a whole new factory to produce the material. But by the mid 19th century, Bradford had become highly polluted from the smoke and grime of its many mills. Salt's solution was to build not just a new mill outside Bradford but a whole new town for his workforce. The site he chose was next to Shipley to the north of Bradford in the Aire valley: he named the new settlement Saltaire.

The mill was built alongside the Leeds and Liverpool Canal between 1851 and 1853, and

ABOVE: The cotton mill built at Fazeley by Sir Robert Peel in 1790 is typical of the period and a very early example of canal-side construction.

was said to be the largest industrial building in the world at that time. It is a handsome structure in the Italianate style and became known as the Palace of Industry. The town was a model of its kind with excellent houses and a wide range of facilities for the locals: an attractive church, library, hospital, almshouses, a public park and school. One notable absentee was a pub. Salt was not opposed to drink as such – he was well known to

Sir Titus Salt not only built a huge factory to manufacture mohair beside the Leeds and Liverpool Canal but also built the whole new town of Saltaire for the workers.

ABOVE: Cash's Topshops beside the Coventry Canal, with workshops for weaving name tags running above the terraced houses.

keep an excellent cellar for himself and guests – but he was determined to prevent his workforce forming any sort of alliance or union. He argued that if they got together in the pub they could start discussing wages and might begin agitating for better conditions – wages in Saltaire were lower than those in Bradford. In fact, all large gatherings were banned, and the towers built into the mill were used to look down on the town and report any large groups of men. It could have created a very discontented workforce, but the excellence of the facilities, far better than in other industrial towns, meant that in general people were satisfied. And conditions were good, and the town well repays a visit. It was also a place full of quirky rules and practices. For example, the front door of your house told everyone your status in the mill. Someone with a four-panel door was higher up the ladder than one with two panels. That did not necessarily mean you got a new house with promotion – just a new front door. Today, the mill houses a shopping complex and the David Hockney Gallery. The other public buildings have also found new uses, but fundamentally Saltaire remains just as it was when it was built over a century and a half ago, with one exception – it now has a pub. It is the most complete, unspoiled example of a new town built to take advantage of canal transport.

Not everything in the textile world was quite straightforward. Coming down the Coventry Canal towards the city centre, one can see a curious building. From this viewpoint, there is what appears to be a perfectly ordinary terrace of Victorian houses, but there is a third storey above that, running the whole length of the row with enormous square windows. The complex is Cash's Topshops. Joseph Cash was a Victorian manufacturer who specialised in producing woven name tapes. He was aware that there had been long periods of discontent among the old hand-loom weavers, who were reluctant to work in the new mills. Cash decided that a large part of the problem was that they had been used to working in their own cottages and disliked going out to work. So he devised his factory, with a block of houses around a central courtyard, above which was the workshop running right round over all the homes. Power came from a steam engine in the yard. At the start of the working day, a whistle was blown and the workers simply went up to the workshop, popping up through trapdoors like demons in a pantomime. Workers no longer appear through hatches, but the company was still weaving name tapes until very recently.

The glass cone towering above the Delph locks on the Stourbridge Canal.

Non-textile industries

Textile mills can be found alongside many of the country's canals, but other industries were more localised. Stourbridge was famous for its glass industry and one of its most important historical remains can be found next to the Stourbridge Canal. The Red House Glass Cone was built around 1790 and remained in use until 1936, when it was owned by Stuart Crystal. The cone itself is an imposing structure, standing 100 feet (30m) high. It is in effect a giant chimney with a furnace at the centre, but it is also the workshop, inside which glass is made. There are openings in the furnace through which the workers can thrust a rod with a globule of glass, then withdraw it and blow down the tube to create a glass bubble. The temperature inside was almost suffocatingly high. I recently visited one of the few sites left in the world where work went on precisely as it had in Stourbridge. It was in Germany, and all the glass-blowers seemed to have bottles of beer at their side. One wonders if the Stourbridge glass-blowers also had a few pints at work or had to make do with water. Their lives were very different from those of the boaters who brought them their raw material.

Salt manufacture was a major industry for Cheshire. The raw material now mostly comes from deep mines, but in the past a good deal of production was based on brine, pumped up from deep underground and then dried at the salt works. The process required a good deal of heat, which in turn demanded large quantities of coal. The Trent and Mersey Canal proved invaluable both in supplying the fuel and in carrying away the finished product. Even as late as the 1890s, a canal site was still considered essential, and one of the few surviving salt works can be seen by the canal at Northwich. Lion Salt Works had a deep brine shaft and pump – in latter years, a 'nodding donkey'. The processing consisted of two phases. The brine was heated in pans under a partial vacuum that reduced the boiling temperature. Once the water had all evaporated, the salt was taken to the drying room for more heating. The works have been restored and are now a museum.

Tom Puddings lined up by the coal hoist at Goole, where they will be picked up and tipped to send the coal into the hold of the coaster. The photograph was taken in the 1970s, and the set-up is no longer in use, though the hoists remain.

Transporting coal

A recurring theme in all the industries described so far is their reliance on coal. Right at the beginning of the canal age, the Duke of Bridgewater had declared that the successful canal would have coal 'at the heel of it'. Transporting coal was vital to the fortunes of many canal companies and in the 19th century important steps were taken to increase efficiency. One of the busiest waterways was the Aire and Calder. In the early 19th century the navigation was extended to a new inland port, Goole. It was usable by sizable coasters and was ideal for the export of coal from the South Yorkshire coalfield. What was required was a method of getting the

coal to the port in large quantities and, once there, unloading it efficiently into the seagoing vessels. The answer was found by William H. Bartholomew.

His idea was to have a train of compartment boats that could be hauled by a steam tug. The individual boats were known as Tom Puddings, because they were just like Yorkshire pudding pans – flat bottomed with straight sides. The typical pan was made of steel, 30 feet (9m) long and 15 feet (4.6m) wide, with a draft of 8 feet (2.4m). When they were strung together, the first boat in the chain had dummy bows attached to reduce water resistance. Up to 17 pans could be used, with a carrying load of over 700 tons, far in excess of any barge able to use the waterway.

Frampton on Severn on the Gloucester and Sharpness Canal. The big concrete structure was part of the Cadbury's (now Cadbury) factory and held chocolate crumb, which would then be sent by water to Bournville.

The problem of conveying large quantities of coal had been solved, but they still had to be unloaded. The answer was a hydraulic hoist. The individual pans were hauled underneath the structure, lifted up and then upturned into a chute that carried the coal down to the hold of the waiting ship. The system was a great success and remained in use well into the second half of the 20th century. I was fortunate enough to see the Tom Puddings in action on the Aire and Calder in the 1970s, and it was fascinating to see how the train was worked through a lock. It was far too long to fit in as a whole, so the train was broken in half, the dummy bows pulled hard against the stern of the tug, and together they went down the lock in the conventional way. That left the rest stranded, and one wondered what would happen next. The lock was refilled, the bottom sluices and the top gate opened and the water simply sucked in the rest of the chain, which could then descend and be reunited. Shortly after that, the service was discontinued. The 20th century saw a new energy source being developed. Large electricity generating stations in Britain mostly worked using steam turbines, which were to become vital customers for collieries. At Ferrybridge, coal came by rail and water, and Ferrybridge B had a grander version of the Goole hoist – a system for upending barges. This was an industrial area where water transport played a vital role until quite recently.

Lighter industries

It was not just heavy industries that relied on water transport. Cadbury had established a factory for making chocolate in central Birmingham in 1847, but by the 1870s they had outgrown it. George Cadbury decided, just as Titus Salt had done, that factories did not have to be in crowded, grimy urban areas. In 1878 he bought a meadow with a trout stream called the Bourn, and the model town of Bournville was born. The new works became known as 'the factory in a garden' and the workforce was housed in a well-planned attractive village. But it was to be the canal network that carried in all the essential ingredients. The factory site was also chosen for its proximity to the Worcester and Birmingham Canal. Condensed milk was made at Frampton on the Gloucester and Sharpness and at Knighton on the Shropshire Union. All three sites carry reminders of those days. The largest complex is inevitably at Bournville itself, with a long wharf backed by canopied warehouses. Knighton factory was used to mix solid blocks of chocolate with milk to make chocolate 'crumb', and here too there is an extensive wharf and warehouse complex. The Cadbury factory at Frampton on Severn is still there but closed in 1982. It is interesting to see that the concern relied on the canals for such a long time, and provided a lucrative trade for the boating community. One boatman made a speciality of carrying the chocolate crumb and became universally known as Chocolate Charlie.

Among Cadbury's successful products was drinking chocolate. But it was not the only hot drink whose production relied on the canals. A Swiss chemist, Dr George Wanders, invented a nutritious drink based on malted barley, which he began manufacturing in 1865. In 1909, it was decided to introduce this new beverage, called Ovamaltine, to Britain, where it became Ovaltine. The site chosen was King's Langley on the Grand Union Canal. Not only did they bring in coal for their furnaces by canal, but they also ran their own fleet of boats, each carrying the company logo.

Not all industries could choose a canal site for their business. Ironworks needed to be near a source of raw material, for example. In the early years, when the only fuel that could be used in the blast furnaces was charcoal, this meant they needed to be situated in wooded areas such as the Weald of Kent. The introduction of coke as a fuel meant that they now needed to be near collieries – and collieries could only exist over coalfields. So choice was restricted, but that did not mean that the ironmasters were unaware of the advantages of canal transport – simply that they needed to find different ways of accessing it. And that is something we shall be looking at in the next chapter.

ABOVE: The Ovaltine factory ran its own fleet of boats on the Grand Union.

CARGO

Coal was always the most important commodity carried on the canals, and the development of industry and industrial towns, combined with the ever-increasing use of steam power, saw production soar during the canal system's busiest years.

Coal production in UK

1700 – 2.7 million tons

1750 – 6.7 million tons

1800 – 10 million tons

1850 – 50 million tons

After 1850, the rapidly developing railways took more and more of the traffic.

PLACES TO VISIT

SALTS MILL, Leeds and Liverpool Canal, Victoria Road, Saltaire BD18 3LA.

TRENCHERFIELD MILL, Leeds and Liverpool Canal, Heritage Way, Wigan WN3 4EF.

CHEDDLETON FLINT MILL, Caldon Canal, Cheadle Road, Cheddleton, Leek ST13 7HL.

MOIRA IRON BLAST FURNACE, Ashby Canal, Furnace Lane, Moira DE12 6AT.

CHAPTER 10

CONNECTING LINKS

Long before the canal age started, industries were laying railed tracks, known as tramways, to connect them to navigable rivers. The greatest concentration connected the collieries of north-east England to the Tyne and the Wear. The earliest versions used wooden rails, but by the middle of the 18th century an improved system was developed using cast iron rails. The wagons were drawn by horses, which meant that the space between the rails had to be kept clear. The sleepers we are accustomed to on modern railways would have tripped them up. Instead, a short rail was supported at each end on a square stone block. A hole was drilled in the centre of the block and filled with a wooden plug into which a metal spike could be driven to hold the rail in place. Even when the rails have long since gone, the stone sleeper blocks remain as evidence of the old system. Tramways were to prove vital to the success of many canals.

Welsh tramways

A good example of the importance of tramways can be found on the Brecon and Abergavenny Canal, though why this should be is not immediately obvious. Indeed, travelling the canal today it is hard to believe it ever had any connection with industry at all. People come for pleasure largely because

LEFT: The tramway ran straight down the wooded hillside and trucks could be run into the warehouse, where the iron they carried would be loaded into boats. The wharfinger's house had windows arranged to provide views of both the tramway incline and the canal.

it is so peaceful, running through the beautiful countryside of the Brecon Beacons National Park. True, there are wharfs and warehouses along the way, but no sign of any industry they might be serving. For most of the route, it simply runs high up on the flank of the Blorenge hill. To solve the mystery, one has to look to the heavily industrialised valleys of South Wales. One site of particular interest can be found at Blaenavon.

A Staffordshire industrialist, Thomas Hill, came here with two associates to establish the Blaenavon ironworks, attracted by the availability of all the raw material he needed. There is still evidence of the local coal industry at the nearby

Big Pit, now a mining museum. The ironworks site is impressive. A row of five massive stone blast furnaces is built against the hillside. Coal, ore and limestone were fed in at the upper level and the molten metal flowed out at the bottom to be cast into moulds to make pig iron. Connecting the two levels was the water balance tower. This is as impressive as the furnaces but works on a simple principle of counterbalancing – a load can be raised to an upper level by adding water to the connected load at the top. The pig iron would be carried up the tower to be shipped away and this is where works and canal became connected.

Hill built his tramway right across the top of the Blorenge mountain, eventually reaching the canal at Llanfoist. On reaching here, the first hint that this is a special place is the flat-topped bridge. Other bridges on the canal are conventionally hump-backed, but this one carried the tracks of Hill's tramway on down to the main road in the valley. Pedestrians wanting to cross the canal had to use a tunnel beneath it – or risk being run down by a loaded truck. From the bridge, a steep path leads up the hillside. Follow that and you soon come across the telltale signs of two parallel rows of

stone sleeper blocks. Further up is a level platform where winding gear once stood, for hauling trucks along the slope.

At the canal, the trucks could be diverted into a warehouse, which is also built out over the water to allow cargo to be exchanged between the tramway trucks and canal boats. The operation was overseen by the wharf manager, whose house stands next to the bridge, with windows providing views of both tramway and canal. This was by no means the only tramway connected to the canal. There is in fact a complex system, with main lines and branch lines leading off to other sites. Another very important route was the Bailey's Tramroad linking the Nantyglo ironworks to the canal at Govilon, with wharf and warehouse. Another connection was made nearby at Gilwern. There is probably no canal in the country served by a more complex system of tramways than the Brecon. It is not, however, the only Welsh canal to be connected by rail to ironworks.

BELOW: Bailey's warehouse at Govilon on the Brecon and Abergavenny Canal. The wharf marked the end of Bailey's Tramroad, which began at the Nantyglo ironworks.

The Glamorganshire Canal was built to join the ironworks of Merthyr Tydfil to the docks at Cardiff. It was, if anything, too successful and boats jostled for position to use the locks between Merthyr and Abercynon. One ironmaster, Samuel Homfray, became frustrated by the delays and promoted a tramway from his Penydarren works to the canal at Abercynon to bypass the locks. It was destined to become famous when in 1804 Homfray invited Richard Trevithick to build a steam locomotive to work on the tramway. It was the first public trial of a railway locomotive ever held. The locomotive itself was a success, but the heavy engine cracked the brittle cast iron rails and it had to be withdrawn. But it marked the start of the railway age and vindicated the Duke of Bridgewater's view that canals would prosper 'If we can keep clear of these damned tramways'. The line of the tramway can still be traced and there is a long section of sleeper blocks in place near Quakers Yard.

BELOW: The canal–rail interchange at Whaley Bridge. Boats from the Peak Forest Canal could float in through the central arch, while waggons from the Cromford and High Peak Railway entered at the opposite end.

North of England tramways

In the north of England, the most extensive tramway remains are to be found on the Peak Forest Canal. The canal received its Act in 1794 and the engineer in charge was Benjamin Outram. He was a great enthusiast for tramways and at the same time as he was developing the canal he was also at work on the Peak Forest Tramway, built to bring limestone to the waterway. The two met at the eastern terminus of the canal, Bugsworth Basin, which has now been restored. This is a magnificent complex and the volunteers who brought it back to life deserve all our thanks. The positions of railway sidings are marked by the lines of stone sleeper blocks, running alongside the basin and the wharfs and out to old lime kilns. The canal structures are also impressive, especially a stone bridge with a cobbled path running across the top. The tramway arrived at the site on an elevated section, carried in a high embankment. In its heyday, as many as 40 boats a day were leaving, loaded with stone or lime. The tramway remained in use until the 1920s.

Bugsworth Basin on the Peak Forest Canal was an important junction between tramway and canal. The tramway embankment can be seen crossing above the wharf area to the left of the picture.

Perhaps the most remarkable tramway was the Cromford and High Peak Railway of 1824 – remarkable because the summit level was almost 1,000 feet (305m) above its starting point on the Cromford Canal. Here there is a wharf and warehouse, with a substantial awning carried on iron pillars. On the side of the building facing Cromford is a wide arched opening leading out to the route of the old tramway. There is now a visitor centre here and among the displays is a section of track laid out as it would have been in working days. The rails are cast iron of the type known as fish-bellied, with a curved underside and mounted conventionally on stone blocks.

This first section simply follows the line of the canal and soon turns off towards the hills. To see how the terrain was conquered, it's necessary to travel away from the canal to Middleton-by-Wirksworth and the Middleton Top engine house. It stands at the top of a steep incline, just one of many along the route. The trucks were hauled up and down the slope by cable, with power supplied by the steam engine. This magnificent machine has been restored by the same volunteers who preserved the Leawood pumping station on the canal. There are regular open days, when the winding engine is demonstrated. Middleton Top is just one of the eight similar stations that were built to carry the lines up from Cromford and down to the Peak Forest Canal at Whaley Bridge. Here the canal–rail interchange building is unusual. There are arched openings in both the end walls, with trucks coming in on rails at one end and boats arriving to float inside at the opposite end.

BELOW: Froghall marks the end of the Caldon Canal. From here, a 3-mile-long (5km) tramway led to the quarries of Caldon Low.

Creative solutions

The tramways were an integral part of the canal system, but are easily overlooked, often because few traces remain. There is very little left now, for example, of the Glyn Ceiriog tramway that once brought slate from mines in the valley to be loaded on to boats at a wharf near the Chirk aqueduct on the Ellesmere Canal. But one tramway of which there are extensive remains is the Haytor Granite Tramway, built in 1820 to carry stone from the quarries high on Dartmoor to the Stover Canal. The situation was remote and shipping in iron rails would have been expensive, so instead 'rails' were constructed from the one material that was readily available – hard-wearing granite. Long lengths can be traced across the moor near the tor, including intriguing points where routes diverged. As it would have been impossible to swing trucks from one set of stone rails to another without some form of help,

metal plates were spiked in place that could be swivelled to allow trucks to change direction.

Tramways were built in terrain where canal construction would have been difficult and often overcame steep slopes by means of cable haulage on inclines. There was, however, an alternative: build inclined planes on canals themselves. Shropshire was one area where there was an abundance of raw material for the iron industry. This was hilly country and if the mines and quarries that supplied coal, ore and stone wanted to deliver by water then a special type of canal was needed. The Shropshire Canal, built between 1788 and 1792 under the direction of William Reynolds, was a tub boat canal. The boats were not unlike the Tom Puddings described earlier, blunt-ended

BELOW: The rails of the tramway along Glyn Ceiriog can be seen in this early 20th-century photograph taken by the aqueduct at Chirk.

iron boxes with flat bottoms. Reynolds had his ironworks at Ketley and it was there he devised his first inclined plane to move the tub boats up and down the slope.

The Ketley incline consisted of a double track of iron rails on which were mounted specially constructed frames, with large wheels at one end and small at the other, so that when placed on the rails the platform would remain level. The tub boat would enter a lock at the top of the incline and water would be let out, allowing the boat to settle down on to the frame. At the same time, a second boat at the bottom of the slope on the adjoining track was floated on to its frame. The two were connected by cables wound round a drum. The top boat with its heavy load was always heavier than the bottom boat so that, as the brake was released on the winding drum, the weight of the descending boat would haul up the empty or partially filled vessel.

One section of the Shropshire Canal runs through the Blists Hill site, part of the Ironbridge Gorge Museums complex. There is an original tub boat here and this section of canal ends at the Hay incline, which has been restored. In operation, it worked like the Ketley incline, but there was also a small steam engine that could be used for haulage when needed. The incline is 1,000 feet (305m) long, with a vertical drop of 207 feet (63m). At the foot of the slope is the Coalport pottery, with its distinctive kiln, and from here a short stretch of the canal leads on to a junction with the River Severn.

Tub boats were also used on the Bude Canal. The first proposal for the canal was made in 1774 but came to nothing and it was only with the formation of a new company in 1819 that the project finally got under way. Its main object was to provide sand from the local beaches to use as a fertiliser to improve the soil inland for agriculture. With its various branches, the canal was 36 miles (58km) long and contained six inclines. Most of

ABOVE: This 1902 photograph of the Trench inclined plane on the Shrewsbury Canal shows how the tub boats were moved on wheeled carriages on the slope.

them were worked by a waterwheel to turn the winding drum. It is still possible to follow the canal from the entrance lock to Helebridge and then continue along the line of the towpath to find the clear line of the first incline, which is 80 feet (24m) long with a rise of 12 feet (3.7m).

Britain's most imposing incline was not built to overcome a difficult terrain, but to ease congestion on a busy canal. The ten locks at Foxton on the Leicester Arm of the Grand Union Canal are arranged in two staircases, each of five locks. They are, however, narrow locks, only able to take in one vessel at a time. With the ever-increasing threat from road and rail transport, the delays caused by boats queuing to use the system were more and more troublesome. The decision was taken to add an inclined plane to speed everything up. This would have to be built on a far greater scale

than anything previously constructed, for it had to be able to carry pairs of narrow boats, not tub boats. Design work went ahead, but before work started on site a complete working model was built at the Bulbourne yard in 1896. The basic idea was to have two caissons, large watertight containers, each able to hold a pair of narrow boats, which would run on railed tracks and would counterbalance each other, though extra power would be supplied by a small steam winding engine. Each caisson was built on a triangular frame to keep it level on the slope and was fitted with wheels running on eight rails per caisson. The boats floated in at one level and off at the other. It was not, however, a great success – largely because of financial difficulties, caused in part by the fact that the engine had to be kept in steam whether needed or not. It closed down in 1911. In recent years, a good deal of restoration work has been carried out and the incline itself is much as it was in working days, apart from not having the caissons, and there is a museum in the former boiler house.

The alternative to the inclined plane was some form of vertical lift. One of the earliest examples, and certainly the oddest, was on the Somerset Coal Canal. Built to link the Radstock collieries to the Kennet and Avon, it has long since been derelict. A short length survives near the Dundas aqueduct, but much of the route can be traced as a footpath that follows the line of the old towpath. Walking the route, there are many remains, but after performing a U-turn, the line of the canal reaches Engine Wood Hill. The name comes from the fact that it was once home to a steam pumping engine and is a section of canal that has seen immense changes.

The problem faced by engineers was how to get the canal up the steep hillside. Robert Weldon was the man who came up with an ingenious solution – the caisson lock. The caisson was a watertight box fitted with doors at both ends. It floated in what was known as the caisson lock, which was in effect a large well. By pumping air into the caisson at the bottom of the lock, it would rise to the upper level – and by pumping air out at the top, it could drop down. The motion was controlled by guide rods. Boats entered the lower level through a short tunnel, floated into the caisson and were then shut in, so that the air could be pumped in. The whole affair then rose and when the upper level was reached the door would be opened and the boat could go on its way. The process was simply reversed for descending boats. It was fine in theory but proved less successful in practice and was soon abandoned. One imagines that the boatmen were relieved not to have their claustrophobic trip up the hillside. The only reminder of those days is a large house at the upper level still known as Caisson House. Although there is little of this early vertical lift to see, it is still an interesting site and one can see the line of the more conventional inclined plane that replaced the caisson lock.

A far more successful system was introduced to the Grand Western Canal by the engineer James Green in the 1830s. Instead of locks, he devised

LEFT: The Hay incline stands at the end of the Shropshire Canal. Tub boats were carried up and down the slope, linking the canal to the River Severn.

BELOW: The Foxton incline photographed at the beginning of the 20th century, showing a pair of narrow boats in a caisson.

a route involving one inclined plane and seven vertical lifts with a total rise of 282 feet (86m). The lifts were complex affairs. Two caissons were suspended from three wheels by wrought iron chains. The caisson at the bottom was jacked against the front wall of the lift to seal it and a door opened at the opposite end to let a boat in. The caisson at the top was similarly jacked but against the back wall. When both boats were in, the doors were closed and the jacks released. The two caissons were now suspended and in balance. Ascent and descent was on the water balance system – water added to the top caisson allowed it to fall, raising

ABOVE: The partially restored Foxton Inclined Plane on the Leicester Arm of the Grand Union. It was built to relieve the pressure on the adjoining locks.

the lower caisson. Although the lifts have long since been discarded and the canal is partially derelict, the Nynehead lift has been excavated by the Canal Trust and gives an excellent idea of the scale of the enterprise.

One 19th-century lift has not only survived but is still in use. In the latter part of the century a major programme was put in hand to improve traffic on the Weaver Navigation under the direction of the engineer Edward Leader Williams. One important commodity produced in the area was salt, and as many of the works were

close to the Trent and Mersey Canal a connection between the two was obviously a good idea. There was, however, just one problem – the difference in level between the two waterways. It was decided that instead of building locks, which would have caused water supply problems for the canal, they should be joined by a vertical lift. In 1872, an Act was passed to approve the construction of a lift that would join the extensive basin at Anderton on the Weaver to the Trent and Mersey.

This is a massive structure that provides a vertical lift of 50 feet (15m). As originally built, it consisted of an iron frame containing two caissons each 75 feet (23m) long, 15ft 6in (4.7m) wide and 5 feet (1.5m) deep, able to take one flat –

the traditional barge of the Weaver – or a pair of narrow boats. A short aqueduct leads out from the Trent and Mersey to the top of the lift, where gates could be closed off to allow the caissons to move freely as watertight tanks. Originally, they were counterbalanced and worked hydraulically. There was always a problem in securing watertight seals between the aqueduct and the caissons. A timber facing was added to the ends of the aqueduct and the troughs, and a rubber sealant added to the former. The caissons were kept moving in a smoothly vertical way by being guided by cast iron blocks running in channels on the frame. Each caisson, weighing 250 tons, was moved by a hydraulic ram. A problem arose after a few years.

The Anderton boat lift, seen here from the River Weaver, was built to carry both barges and narrow boats between the river and the Trent and Mersey Canal above it.

The hydraulic system used water that was heavily polluted by the effluent from chemical works round Anderton. The result was that it rotted the sealants and the resulting leakage caused one catastrophic collapse. An improvement was made by condensing the exhaust steam from auxiliary engines for the hydraulics, but by 1902 it was decided to abandon hydraulics and turn to electric power.

Under the new system, the caissons were no longer counterbalanced, but operated independently, which greatly increased the efficiency of the system. However, some form of counterbalance was still needed, and the answer was to suspend a series of weights that hang from the frame, giving the whole structure a slightly bizarre appearance. The lift continued running satisfactorily well into the latter part of the 20th century, at which point major restoration work was needed. In 1997, the operation returned to hydraulics, though without the problems that had beset the Victorian machinery. Today, the lift is still in use and has become a popular visitor attraction.

In recent years, the canal restoration movement has seen many old waterways that had once been derelict brought back to life, and among the more successful schemes was the reuniting of two major canals in Scotland – the Forth and Clyde and the Edinburgh and Glasgow Union. Originally, they had been joined by a flight of eleven locks with a total rise of 115 feet (35m); however, it was decided not to rebuild these but instead to build just two locks at the upper level and go for a more dramatic solution – a boat lift at Falkirk to deal with the remaining difference in levels. Engineering solutions can be very basic, but the new structure built here is not only a practical machine but an object of great beauty – the Falkirk Wheel. The idea is not unlike a giant Ferris wheel, where the passenger compartments are attached to the wheel but always remain horizontal as the wheel turns, except that in this case, instead of small passenger cabins, large caissons move with the wheel. It is not an easy concept to grasp when you're talking about moving boats, but the chief architect on the project used a very homely

BELOW: A modern engineering marvel: the Falkirk Wheel boat lift, built to replace the flight of locks that once joined the Forth and Clyde and Edinburgh and Glasgow Union canals.

material to build his demonstration models – Lego.

In some ways, the system is not unlike that at Anderton, with two counterbalanced caissons, the top level approached via the two locks and a short aqueduct and the lower straight from the canal. The method of movement, however, is dramatically different. The caissons rest on wheeled bogies running inside giant rings, automatically finding their own level. As a result, they remain horizontal as the wheel turns, one ascending on one side through a semicircular path, while the other is a mirror image as it descends. This great structure was completed to mark the millennium and it is as powerful a symbol of this canal age as any of the great structures of the past. It is as elegant in operation as it is in appearance. There is, however, a link with the past. The steel wheel was manufactured at the Butterley works in Derbyshire, which had supplied iron for canal structures two centuries ago, when the works were founded by William Jessop and Benjamin Outram. Not every structure added to the canal scene in recent years has been so beneficial, but at the same time much has happened to revive the system, which had suffered years of neglect.

PLACES TO VISIT

BUGSWORTH BASIN, Peak Forest Canal, Buxworth, High Peak SK23 7NE.

HAY INCLINE, Shropshire tub boat canal, Blists Hill Museum, Telford TF8 7HY.

ANDERTON BOAT LIFT, Trent and Mersey Canal, Lift Lane, Anderton, Northwich CW9 6FW.

FALKIRK WHEEL BOAT LIFT, Forth and Clyde Canal, Lime Road, Tamfourhill FK1 4RS.

TRAMWAY WORKING

The following account of one of the Brecon and Abergavenny tramways is taken from the Duke of Rutland's account of a journey through Wales, published in 1805.

'This rail-road is adapted to the size of the waggons to be used, or carts, which convey the coal to the canal. On each side is an iron groove which extends the whole length of the road, and on which the wheels (four or six in number) run. They are so contrived as to run downwards the whole way (sometimes for the extent of some miles) from the works; so that when laden, they require no horses to draw them down. Indeed they acquire so great a degree of velocity in their descent, that a man is forced to walk or run behind the cart, with a kind of rudder or pole affixed to the hind-wheel, which he locks up when it proceeds too fast. Should this pole break (which it sometimes does) the waggon flies away, and overturns everything it meets. Of course, any one who is coming up the road, is in imminent danger, unless he can by any means get out of the way; which is very difficult, as the road is narrow and runs along a precipice. Last year, Mr. Frere the proprietor of the ironworks, was returning from London, and going along the rail-road in a post-chaise, when about a hundred yards from him, he saw one of those waggons coming down upon him with astonishing velocity. He could not possibly get out of the way, and must have been crushed to pieces, if fortunately the waggon had not broken over the iron groove, which had hitherto kept it in the track, and run forcibly up an ash tree by the side of the road, in the branches of which it literally stuck, and thus saved him from immediate destruction.'

The aqueduct that leads to the top of the Falkirk Wheel.

CHAPTER 11

A CHANGING WORLD

The first half of the 20th century saw a period of decline in canal traffic, faced by the dual challenge of railways and motor transport on the roads. Only the most prosperous routes survived, and many canals were abandoned. By the second half of the century, commercial carrying was virtually over, certainly as far as the narrow canals were concerned. But at the same time a new trade was developing in holiday boating. The emphasis was shifting from improving efficiency to preserving the historic nature of the waterways. New uses were found for old buildings: warehouses could be converted to a variety of new purposes from museums to retail centres; wharfs and basins now provided homes for pleasure boats. One type of building, however, did not really need to find a new use – the canal pub could just as happily serve pints to holidaymakers as it once had to working boaters.

Boating community hubs

It is tempting to think that the canal-side pub has remained just as it has been for centuries, but of course that is not really the case. Even if the exterior remains largely unaltered, the interior will probably have seen many changes. In the working days of the canals, the pub was something much more than somewhere to drop in for a pint and a pie: it was a vital social centre. For communities constantly on the move, it was the place where boating families could meet friends and relations – and the young could get to know each other. And many of the pubs also acted as shops, selling essential supplies. Junctions were always popular meeting places, and The Greyhound at Hawkesbury Junction, meeting place of the Oxford and Coventry canals, was typical. Like most canal pubs, it had no need to provide fancy architectural embellishments to attract customers, but was built in the common vernacular for pubs in the region. It is comparatively large, having been built in 1825 when business on the two canals was booming. Also, like most other canal pubs, the interior has been much altered to meet changing tastes, but

LEFT: The Greyhound at Hawkesbury Junction was always a great meeting place for boating families.

the snug bar is still redolent of older times.

There were some, however, where a regular trade was assured. Most canal tunnels had no towpath, so boats were legged through. Legging was hard work and built up a healthy thirst, while at the same time there were often delays as boats waited for their turn – and the pub was as good a place as any to while away the time. The Tunnel End Inn at Marsden on the Huddersfield Narrow must have enjoyed a particularly good trade, standing at the end of Britain's longest tunnel. One unlikely tunnel traveller was Buttercup, not a boat but a cow that fell into the canal at one end of Foulridge Tunnel on the Leeds and Liverpool, swam through the whole mile and was revived at the Hole in the Wall pub at the other end. Sadly, she would not receive the treatment today – the pub has closed.

Wherever there were wharfs and canal-side settlements, there was likely to be a pub. The boat community were not simply responsible for moving cargo from place to place, they normally had the job of loading and unloading as well. Shovelling out tons of coal from boat to wharf is thirsty work. The Boat Inn at Stoke Bruerne, for example, was always going to do well, as there was a small settlement here with a warehouse, and it is very near the start of the long Blisworth Tunnel. It is unusual in having a very countrified appearance, including a thatched roof. The Admiral Nelson, further along the Grand Union at Braunston, is far more typical, a very plain building, but enjoying a most attractive setting beside a lock.

RIGHT: The Admiral Nelson at Braunston was actually a farmhouse before the Grand Junction Canal came along and it found a new role as a pub.

BELOW: The Grove Lock on the Grand Union – the name tells you exactly where it is, though we cannot always have the pleasure of seeing a genuine old working boat using the lock.

The Globe at Linslade is one of the most attractive waterside pubs.

One could go on listing attractive pubs, but one thing would soon become obvious: many of them have telltale names. Boats and Ships proliferate and names with nautical connections are common. If you see a pub called The Anchor miles from the sea, you can be fairly sure it stands near a waterway. The signs can even be informative. The Ship Inn near the basin at Brimscombe Port on the Thames and Severn Canal, for example, has a sign showing a Severn trow, a reminder that these sailing barges could once have been regular visitors from the river. And it is not just signs that are informative. The Navigation at Bugsworth Basin has a wealth of old photos of the working days of the site and canal memorabilia.

It is perhaps a little misleading to think that all canal pubs were like these survivors. Many were no more than everyday houses, from which beer was sold. Until a few years ago, there was a pub called The Bird in Hand at Kent Green, which had a beer-only licence; one walked in to what appeared to be someone's living room and the landlady would go down to the cellar to fill a jug with beer. When the canals were new, many pubs would have been this basic.

BELOW: An attractively appropriate sign on the Rochdale Canal at Chadderton.

Today's canal environment

Today, new pubs have opened, some specially built, others created out of old canal buildings. It is a mark of the growing appreciation of canals as places where it is enjoyable to spend one's time. This has been true for a long time of rural canals, but it took time for the urban canals to be appreciated in the same way. Nowhere has seen a greater transformation than Birmingham. Those of us who first boated extensively on the Birmingham system decades ago found ourselves in a rather secret world, shut off entirely from the everyday life of the city. If the canals were regarded at all, it was as useful places to dump rubbish.

The first glimpse of what an urban canal could be came in the 1970s. Cambrian Wharf originally marked the southern end of the Brindley version of the Birmingham Canal. This was to be the first attempt to renovate an area such as this and the work was carried out very sympathetically. Old buildings, including a row of 18th-century cottages, were refurbished and the cobbled wharf was spruced up with the old hand cranes retained, now seeming more like waterside sculpture than practical machines. And to attract visitors a new

BOAT AND HORSES

canal-side pub, The Longboat, was built. It was never perhaps the most exciting building but it had the virtue of looking out over the canal and had moorings right outside. It is still there but has now been given the strange name of Flapper and Firkin, as though the new owners were somehow ashamed to admit its links with the canal. However, the whole scheme attracted a lot of attention and demonstrated that there was much to be gained by enjoying a pint while looking out over the water, seeing the occasional passing boat. Canals could be attractive and, what was important for later developments, could bring paying customers to the area. The success of the scheme led to its receiving a Civic Trust award. The architect responsible for developing the scheme for the city council was

ABOVE: The restoration of the old canal-side buildings marked the start of the realisation that Birmingham's canals were a huge asset.

Peter White, who shortly afterwards joined British Waterways as their chief architect. There, he was to apply the same principles of robust yet sensitive development that made the most of the existing canal structures.

The decades following the Cambrian Wharf scheme were to see the canal scene in Birmingham change dramatically; new buildings appeared and what had once been quiet backwaters were now crowded with bars and restaurants. The Brindley Place scheme typifies the new atmosphere, now teeming with people enjoying the ambience.

Brindley Place epitomises the way in which Birmingham has now turned to its canals – an area lined with bars and restaurants.

The transformation was not limited to Birmingham. In London, the canal had always been regarded as an asset rather than a liability, at least in some parts of the system. The Regent's Canal basin at Little Venice became the heart of one of the more fashionable areas of the city, and the fact that the canal passed close to Regent's Park and the zoo made it a popular route for trip boats.

But in recent times, other sections have also been popular. The area round Camden Locks has sprouted a hugely popular market. It is housed in the former goods depot, built for the London and Birmingham Railway, and sited beside the canal to make the interchange of goods as efficient as possible. Visitors not only come in their thousands to the market with its stalls and restaurants, but many wander out to watch boats using the lock, just enjoying the canal scene. This is not a new phenomenon: even back in the 19th century, people were fascinated by seeing boats at work, and they earned themselves a special name in the canal vocabulary – gongoozlers.

The other interesting development in Camden Town saw the erection of new housing beside the water. In an area mostly noted for the use of London stock brick, these metal-clad buildings stood out as almost startlingly modern. Today they seem perfectly acceptable and, as with many

BELOW: Little Venice has always been a fashionable area of London that has made the most of having the Regent's Canal at its heart.

RIGHT: Unlike Little Venice, the area round Camden Locks has only recently become a tourist destination, largely due to the very successful market.

new buildings, the use of steel and glass provides a new element of ever-changing reflections from the water. They are preferable to the pastiche, 'traditional' houses that are appearing on too many canal sites. This is the other side of the coin: once it had been established that people actually valued a canal site, it was an invitation for developers to step in, who simply built what was easiest to build and quickest to sell with little regard for the situation.

Other sites have been developed in London, and turned into much valued public amenities, such as Paddington Basin. More cities have followed suit, such as Leeds and Manchester, but it would be tedious to cover them all in detail. But few who travelled the Rochdale Canal in the old days

would ever have imagined that Canal Street would be the heart of a vibrant gay scene. Urban canal regeneration is one of the most dramatic changes to the canal scene, but equally important has been the restoration of once derelict waterways.

RIGHT TOP: Leeds is another city that has seen substantial developments taking advantage of the canal's attractions.

RIGHT BOTTOM: Paddington Basin has been transformed in recent years and one of its more attractive additions is the rolling bridge, which actually curls up rather than rolls.

BELOW: At King's Cross, the Regent's Canal has become a theatre with boats as the performers, enjoyed by the spectators on the tiered seating.

Recently, the Leeds and Liverpool Canal has been brought right into the heart of Liverpool; this boat is approaching the iconic Liver Building on the right and the new Liverpool Museum to the left.

The restoration movement had its first success with the southern section of the Stratford-upon-Avon Canal. An application to abandon the neglected waterway was made in 1959 on the grounds that not a single boat had been down it for years. But someone had – a canoeist was able to provide proof that he had travelled the whole length, and the application was rejected. The National Trust acquired the canal, and a team was assembled that included the Stratford Canal Society and the newly formed Inland Waterways Association to restore the canal under the direction of David Hutchings. As a result, the canal was opened and back in use in 1964. Other, far more demanding undertakings also got under way, including the restoration of major waterways such as the Kennet and Avon and Basingstoke canals. In the early years, much of the work was done by volunteers, who were prepared to take on the most unsavoury jobs. The author recalls working at Deepcut on the Basingstoke, pushing a barrowload of silt from the bottom of a lock, out along a greasy plank. The barrow slipped off the greasy wood and began to disappear under the mud; it was only just rescued before it vanished from sight.

LEFT TOP: Volunteers at work in the mud at Deepcut on the Basingstoke Canal in 1976.

LEFT BOTTOM: A new bridge under construction on the Basingstoke Canal in the 1970s. The technology remains the same as when the first bridges were built here two centuries earlier.

BELOW: The first major restoration scheme was on the Stratford Canal. The canal basin is watched over by William Shakespeare and four of his characters. Lady Macbeth and Falstaff are seen here.

The main aim of most restorers was to bring a canal back to its original condition, but that was not always possible. On the Kennet and Avon, for example, locks 8 and 9 in Bath had to be merged to create a single deep lock, due to changes in the road that crosses the flight. The new lock is 19 feet 5 inches (6m) deep, and boaters found their mooring lines didn't always reach the top, and their boats were bumping around as the water flowed in or out. Vertical rails were added to the

ABOVE: Spectators gather to watch boats pass through the newly restored Deep Cut locks on the Basingstoke Canal.

RIGHT: When restoration began on the Kennet and Avon Canal, a road had been built over the two locks at the start of the Bath flight. The answer was to make one new, very deep lock.

lock wall, around which the lines could be looped, and peace was restored. Other schemes required more drastic action.

Two of the biggest schemes undertaken were to restore the two trans-Pennine routes, the Huddersfield and Rochdale canals. By the time work got under way on these, although volunteers still played a vital role, the work could only be completed by raising huge sums of money to employ professionals. Among the major problems on the Huddersfield was the fact that a large part of the canal had been built over in Slaithwaite near Huddersfield. So, an entirely new section was built through the town. It has been beautifully done and one can scarcely believe it wasn't built when the canal was brand new. A similar problem came during the restoration of the Thames and Severn in Stroud. A town centre bypass runs beneath an arch of the railway viaduct, once occupied by the canal. Again, a whole new section of canal had to be built. This project, however, faces an even greater obstacle. It was not just an ordinary road that has been built over the canal, but the M5 has obliterated it. The proposal is to go under the embankment, requiring major engineering works.

The canal network is now more widespread than it has been for more than half a century, and on a summer's day there are probably more craft on the move than there were 100 years ago.

ABOVE: The new section of the Huddersfield Narrow Canal runs through the heart of Slaithwaite.

It is a remarkable fact that a transport system built up to serve industry and shareholders, but which has long since been overtaken by more modern transport systems, should still be in use at all. That it is so is no accident. We are fortunate that the men who designed our canals lived in an age that many regard as being the pinnacle of architectural excellence. That almost innate sense of good proportion seems to have seeped through from the domestic to the practical realm. We are also lucky that before canals came along, transport in Britain was in a woeful state, so wherever possible purely local materials were used. Canals sit comfortably in their very local landscapes. We have a magnificent legacy and one that is of great historic importance. The Industrial Revolution that began in Britain in the middle of the 18th century spread out from these shores and changed the world for ever. And it could never have happened without the canals that were its life blood. It is up to us and future generations to preserve this magnificent heritage.

Index

Acknowledgements

All the photographs in the book are by Derek Pratt with the following exceptions:
Anthony Burton 168 (bottom), 178, 188
Bodleian Library, University of Oxford 91 (bottom)
British Museum 13
British Waterways Archive 28, 66, 91 (top), 122, 123, 146 (top), 187, 189, 191
Josiah Wedgwood & Sons Ltd 159–160
Museum of London 88
Oxfordshire County Libraries 18

Flower detail artwork by Louise Turpin

ABOVE: A barrel-vaulted lock cottage on the Stratford Canal.